Roseanne Harvey, Larry Brown & Joel Katelnikoff

COMING ATTRACTIONS
06

We acknowledge the support of the Canada Council for the Arts, the Government of Ontario through the Ontario Media Development Corporation and the Government of Canada through the Book Publishing Industry Development Program for our publishing activities.

An excerpt from "Between Stops" by Roseanne Harvey first appeared in *subTerrain*. "Pin Girl" by Larry Brown was first published in *The Malahat Review*. "Skin" by Larry Brown first appeared in *The New Quarterly*. "The Right Pieces" by Larry Brown originally appeared in *The Fiddlehead*. "Notes on the Apocalypse" by Joel Katelnikoff was first published in *Grain*. The untitled robot story by Joel Katelnikoff was originally published in *The Antigonish Review*.

ISBN 0 7780 1288 3 (hardcover)
ISBN 0 7780 1289 1 (softcover)

Cover art by Hansi
Book design by Michael Macklem

Printed in Canada

PUBLISHED IN CANADA BY OBERON PRESS

Canada Council   Conseil des Arts
for the Arts   du Canada

Contents

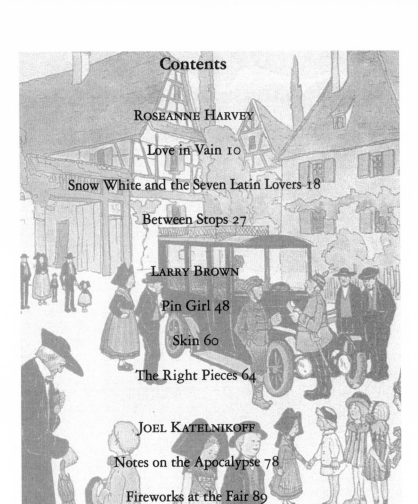

HERE'S A TOAST to the leaves of summer and to the crisp light of autumn pouring in a window, and here's a toast to the fierce pleasures of reading three crisp new writers: Joel Katelnikoff, Larry Brown and Roseanne Harvey.

The word quirky is dead from overuse, but it's a word that fits Joel Katelnikoff's utterly unique voice. This Saskabush boy, now living in Edmonton, is impressively idiosyncratic; his stories are never dull. He has been involved for years with the underground zine scene, worships Snoop Dog, and spends too much of his time observing large sweaty men wrestling each other in tiny panty-like outfits. Sometimes I think he is from some other solar system that is very similar to the one I move about in; sometimes I think he is a genius. Read him and weep.

Larry Brown, the pride of Brantford, writes stories that are jittery and tough; measured, terse prose reminiscent of American authors like Hubert Selby or Ray Carver. His characters are up to skullduggery, yet they are oddly likeable—Brown is adept at making them understandable—and there are admirable qualities of humour ("Shorts, he wanted them") and affection in his treatment of the troubled actors stalking his slightly skewed stage. He is published in many quarterlies, but Brown doesn't waste a word.

Roseanne Harvey, who has spent time in a BC ashram and now lives in Montreal, sets her stories in a Japanese theme park, a weird representation of the whole world, a Babel with southern blues singers set in wax, a Russian calliope, and an Eiffel Tower hard by the Great Wall of China—a twilight universe that is painstakingly realistic, and yet dreamlike, oppressive, haunting.

Three new writers of massive promise and talent and charm, dedicated to reinterpreting our weird world and nailing down mysteries of the psyche.

MARK ANTHONY JARMAN

Contributions for Coming Attractions 07, *published or unpublished, should be sent to Oberon Press, 205–145 Spruce Street, Ottawa, Ontario* K1R 6P1 *before 31 March, 2007. All manuscripts should enclose a stamped self-addressed envelope.*

ROSEANNE HARVEY

Love in Vain

At the end of the day Kaname walks through the wax museum, turning out the lights and checking temperature controls. The museum is just twenty degrees Celsius, exactly where it should be. It feels cooler, because of the darkness. The environment has to be monitored to ensure the wax doesn't melt, warp or discolour. This is the best part of the day for Kaname and he walks slowly, savouring every detail of each figure.

He stands for a few minutes in front of his favourite effigies: Leonardo DiCaprio and Kate Winslet on the *Titanic*, the Beatles, and Lady Diana. Kaname has spent hours in front of Lady Diana, admiring the life-like quality of her skin and the shine of her hair. Taka-sensei, the museum's former wax figure designer whom Kaname apprenticed under, had hand-sewn each strand of real human hair into Lady Di's head. The lighting reflects off her hair and shines around her—like a halo Kaname thinks. He reaches across the rope and brushes a piece of hair that had fallen out from under Lady Diana's tiara. Her forehead feels cold and dry, almost like paper. Kaname is reminded of his mother's skin, matte and poreless like Lady Di's.

At the end of the hallways lined with wax life forms is the west wing, which will open to the public tomorrow evening with an invite-only black tie event. The seven figures within are Kaname's first significant contribution to the museum. Taka-sensei had a plan for the wing but kept it top secret. When he suddenly passed away six months into Kaname's apprenticeship, Kaname was left with the project. Taka-sensei had started seven forms in the design studio but left no information about what shape these would take. Kaname suspected that Taka-sensei's top-secret plan involved scenes from samurai dramas. Taka-sensei had a collection of swords and belonged to some sort of samurai club.

Kaname, however, knew nothing about samurai dramas and had no interest in recreating scenes from old movies. Do whatever you want, museum management told him. So Kaname spent four years creating a wax tribute to his favourite blues musicians. He flicks on the lights in the west wing and imagines introducing Snow White to the first musician. "This is Howlin' Wolf," he would say to her. The figure is a middle-aged black man holding a guitar, his head thrown back in laughter. This is what Kaname loves about Howlin' Wolf, this laughter that comes through even though he's singing the blues.

Imagining Snow White by his side, Kaname walks slowly through the rest of the west wing, which he calls 'The Crossroads' in his mind. He walks past John Lee Hooker, in sunglasses and a black hat, leaning back in a chair. John Lee Hooker's wax arms are wrapped around his guitar, his white fingernails so bright against dark fingers adorned in gold rings. Lightnin' Hopkins sits with an acoustic guitar balanced on his lap and a huge cigar in his right hand. Kaname isn't a fan of Bo Diddley's repetitive rhythms and lack of chord changes, but he likes Diddley's style, his horn-rimmed glasses and little cigar box-shaped guitar. A wax BB King in a shiny gold jacket plays on a replica of Lucille. The only effigy not holding a guitar is Muddy Waters. The figure is based on the image on the cover of "Hard Again," where Muddy Waters' hands are shoved in his pockets and he seems to giggle mischievously.

At the end of the west wing, just before the exit, is the effigy Kaname is the most proud of. He spent eight months designing Robert Johnson, based on a photo taken in 1932. In the image, Robert Johnson sits with his guitar resting on crossed legs. He's wearing a suit and hat, the strong fingers of his left hand hold a firm bar chord. This is one of only two remaining pictures of Robert Johnson. The other photo was taken in a photo booth, Robert Johnson holding his guitar, a cigarette hanging out of his mouth. Kaname would tell

Snow White how Robert Johnson disappeared from Mississippi for a period of time and is believed to have made a pact with the devil in exchange for his guitar-playing ability. Would Snow White be fascinated by this? Would she want to know the whole story, every last detail about Robert Johnson and these other musicians?

This afternoon, Kaname had noticed Snow White as he walked past the German Village on his way back from the staff cafeteria. The wax museum is on the third floor of the Eiffel Tower in European Village, the entire continent crammed into the northwest corner of Wonder World. Snow White walked around the entrance of the German Village, holding a basket and talking to children. Her long black hair hung loose around her shoulders, framing her face and her white white skin, and she wore a long velvet dress and black Mary Jane shoes. It was her skin that made Kaname stop, the air rising out of his lungs and his head suddenly light. As he walked by the entrance, Snow White handed him a pamphlet for the wooden roller-coaster and her fingers brushed across his palm. The warmth and softness of her skin startled him.

Kaname has little experience with women's skin. His mother tried to introduce him to some of her clients from the beauty salon and young women in her weekly English conversation group. She organized meetings at local restaurants or afternoon outings to cultural events. Kaname was polite and friendly to the women, but he usually slipped away before the end of the evening or event. Finally, he asked his mother to stop her attempts at matchmaking.

"Don't you want to be with somebody?" she asked.

He shrugged. "Not like that."

"But you've never even brought home a girl to meet me. Are you ashamed of your family?"

Kaname peered out from behind his mop of thick shaggy hair at their tiny kitchen and dining area, his grandparents watching TV in the living-room, the sliding doors out the balcony. How could he tell her that there just were no girls?

"I don't know what your problem is," his mother said. "Or what you do when you're not at home. But at least you aren't like Tono-chan." Tono-chan lived with his family across the street. His mother and sister got their hair done at Kaname's mother's salon. Tono-chan dropped out of high school and hadn't left his bedroom in over a year, spending all of his time playing computer games and watching TV.

Kaname thinks about the crystal clear blue of Snow White's eyes, her long eyelashes and the freckles across her nose. Her skin so white, looking so soft. He walks between the European Village and the staff cafeteria at least twice a day, and yet he'd never noticed her before. What is this feeling? And why is this happening today? Why not yesterday or tomorrow or any other day? The brief encounter with this fairytale girl with skin like white chocolate. Why has he never seen her before?

As he thinks about Snow White's perfect white skin and her eyes like tiny globes, luminescent as crystal balls, Kaname remembers the first time he met Taka-sensei. On Kaname's first day of work at the wax museum, the director took him to the studio and introduced him to a man curled around a hairless and unidentifiable wax head.

"Taka-sensei, this is your apprentice," the director said, shuffling his feet and laughing slightly. With a polite bow, Kaname recited his memorized introduction: "I am Kaname. I have just finished the art program at Kyoto University, where I focused on wax sculpture. I look forward to learning from you. Yoroshiku onegaishimasu."

Taka-sensei looked up, grunted a greeting, and went back to positioning a glass eyeball in the wax face. Most of Kaname's sculpture work involved wax. For his classes, he carved intricate animals with big dewy eyes. He thought he was destined for a career in the art world and never would have imagined himself working at a wax museum in a theme park. Since he graduated from university, he's stopped making his own art. But he's glad to spend his working days handling wax, which he loves because it's malleable and submissive. Nothing else in his life can be moulded with his touch.

Over the following months, Kaname got to know Taka-sensei and learned that his life was like a blues song: all whiskey, women and work. This was one of the many things he admired about his teacher. Taka-sensei fostered in Kaname a love of blues music. He brought records to Kaname, carefully cared-for discs of thick black vinyl, and told him stories about the men who played the music.

Kaname owns all of the 42 tracks that Robert Johnson recorded in his short career. He has several boxed sets of CDs, as well as a stack of records left to him in Taka-sensei's will. Kaname owns a lot of vinyl. His small bedroom in his mother's apartment is full of stereo equipment, electric guitars and records. He loves sliding a record out of its sleeve, holding it by the edges and setting it on the turntable, then placing the needle at the beginning of the first track.

Taka-sensei was the closest person to a father in Kaname's life. His real father, a salaryman who worked for Sony, died of a heart attack when Kaname was two years old. His mother moved in with her ageing parents and supported the four of them by working at the beauty salon below the apartment. She never remarried and has had no serious relationships since her husband died. Kaname was 22 when he met Taka-sensei and he wondered how he could have lived so long without knowing a father.

The opening chords of "Love in Vain," in Johnson's plucky style, run through Kaname's head as he stands in front of the wax figure. "I'm so lonesome," he whispers. "I'm so lonesome, I could surely die." He hums the chorus and ponders the meaning of the words: love in vain. What does it mean to love somebody in vain? Is that what will happen with Snow White? Will he just end up loving her in vain?

The west wing is as much a tribute to the man who taught Kaname everything he knows about wax statues and blues music as it is to the legends he loves. Taka-sensei also taught Kaname everything he knows about women. Kaname noted the parallels between the women in Taka-sensei's life and the women in blues songs. Women are always loving and leaving, breaking hearts, driving men to whiskey. He thinks about Willie Mae in "Love in Vain," just getting on the train and leaving Robert Johnson with his suitcase on the platform.

One evening after work, Taka-sensei and Kaname drank pints of beer at a Parisian-style bar near the tower. "Robert Johnson was poisoned," Taka-sensei announced. "Whiskey. Some tavern owner poisoned his whiskey because Robert Johnson was going after his woman." Taka-sensei often warned Kaname of the consequences of going after another man's woman. He didn't seem to notice that Kaname didn't even go after single women.

The only woman Kaname has ever spent a lot of time with is his mother. People have often mistaken Kaname and his mother for brother and sister. He resembles his mother, sharing the same facial structure and fine nose. His mother once had high and delicate cheekbones like his, but the muscles in her face have slackened and her skin has lost some of its elasticity. She still strives for these cheekbones, tries to create an illusion of definition with shading and blush. Kaname's face is usually hidden under his thick mop of shaggy black hair, which seems to act as a filter between him and the world. Since he was in junior high, Kaname has styled his hair like Joey Ramone. He was a big Ramones fan for a few years and although he outgrew the music he never became tired of the style. He has worn black jeans and black Chuck Taylor All-Stars since his junior high days, frustrating his mother. She tried to introduce him to different clothing styles, but he politely refused the big T-shirts, trendy running shoes and baggy pants she bought for him.

Kaname takes a deep breath, looks around the museum one last time and shuts off the lights. He walks through the gift shop back to the ticket booth, ensures the cash box is safe and lets himself out to the third floor lobby. At the elevator, he presses the 'up' button. Usually he goes down, walks twenty minutes to the main entrance of the theme park and catches the 6.41 train into the city, to the apartment above his mother's beauty salon, where rice and miso soup will be waiting for him. But today, for some reason Kaname doesn't even understand, he goes down.

The elevator doors open and a robotic feminine voice greets him with "Irashaimase!!" He steps inside and presses the button for the sixth floor. In a few seconds, the voice chirps "Roku-gai desu!!" and Kaname steps out onto the observation deck of the Eiffel Tower. The observation deck is closed in; a thin layer of glass separates him from the world. The window faces west and Kaname can see all of Wonder World, the size of a small city, stretching toward the mountains and the setting sun. He can see the wooden roller-coaster, curled up like a fetus in a womb. Beyond the roller-coaster, Kaname sees the Great Wall of China, the Egyptian pyramids and miniature Mount Kilimanjaro. How could such a small country contain such a big world, he wonders.

Reaching into his back pocket, Kaname pulls out the pamphlet that Snow White had handed him, a photo of a roller coaster and short description about the real wooden roller coaster in Germany that it's based on. Kaname had no idea there was a roller coaster in European Village. He has actually been nowhere in Wonder World except the staff cafeteria and the pub around the corner from the Eiffel Tower. Every day he walks past the entrances to Greece, England and Italy, but has never entered.

What is it about her? Kaname holds the pamphlet to his face and breathes in the soft warmth of her hand. Their eyes locked, he felt it. He has no idea how long their eyes held.

Time stopped, or else it sped up. Now what happens, Kaname wonders. This happened and what happens next? He looks at the picture of the wooden roller-coaster, twisted and wound around itself. He feels like he is in the front car, at the top of the highest peak, about to take a plunge.

Kaname watches the sun slide behind the mountains. To the north, he can see the five points of the dai character carved into the mountain overlooking Kyoto. He wonders if she's riding the train which snakes across the rows of suburban streets toward the city, wonders where she lives and what she is doing this evening. It's hard to tell, so hard to tell. Kaname folds the pamphlet into an origami crane, thinks about form folding into form and shaping his world with the touch of his fingers, then places the crane on the ledge of the observation deck window.

Snow White and the Seven Latin Lovers

Colette takes a place at the row of mirrors along the wall and looks at her reflection in the mirror: purple velvet dress, long black wig, the makeup on her face starting to wear off. Jesus Christ, she thinks. On her left, Cleopatra traces a line around her eyes with a charcoal pencil, and in the corner, the Little Mermaid adjusts her tail then attacks her hair with a curling iron. Gretchen, cloaked in her Little Red Riding Hood outfit, skips out of a change stall and lands at the mirror on Colette's right.

"Hello, princess," Gretchen says, smiling at Colette's reflection in the mirror. "Are you finishing work early? Aren't you supposed to get off at four?" Gretchen is here for the two o'clock shift; Colette has been here since ten.

"I can't take it anymore," Colette says, pouring make-up remover onto a small cotton pad. "My head is throbbing. I can't talk to people. I'm useless out there. I told Hayashi-san that I'm sick and need to go home."

"You always do that," says Gretchen, painting her eyelashes thick with mascara. "The last I saw of you last night, you were salsa dancing with that Spanish guy." The two women and some of their German Village co-workers had been at the Wonder World nightclub for staff appreciation night. Cheap highballs and free shots for theme park staff, no access for guests. Thursday nights at the club are the most genuinely international time at the theme park. "Is he the same guy you met last week?"

"No, that was Ferdinand. He was celebrating his last night in Japan. This guy—" Colette leans into the mirror, smearing the cotton pad across her face, removing the white powder, the shadow caked onto her eyes. "What was his name? Enrique? Eric? Something like that. He's Don Quixote in the Spanish park."

"Another red hot wild stallion Latin lover," Gretchen sighs.

"It was the way he said it: Key-ho-te. That's when I knew I'd sleep with him." Colette soaks another cotton pad and rubs it across her face, getting rid of the last traces of make-up. Her skin is blotchy and red; her eyes look squinty, as if she'd just woken up. She feels that way too. Everyday as she's getting off work, she feels like she's waking up from a dream. "I'm getting too old to be waking up in somebody else's bed. Or futon, as the case may be. All I know is that I woke up next to a sleeping Spaniard in the staff accommodations on the other side of the theme park, threw on my clothes and came straight to work." This is the seventh time this has happened in the three months since she came to Japan.

"It must be some strange form of culture shock," offers Gretchen. "If it wasn't for Joachim, I'd be doing the same thing."

"Instead, you work out obsessively and have a huge long-distance phone bill." Colette pulls the wig off her head. Her long blond hair is braided and wrapped around itself in a loose bun. She undoes the elastics and runs her fingers through her hair, combing out the braid. Colette turns around and opens the locker behind her. She grabs her jeans and sparkly tank top, which smell of smoke and liquor and male sweat. "God, Gretchen," she says, dropping them on the floor. "I can't wear this."

"I just came from the gym," says Gretchen. "You can borrow my work-out clothes." She pulls a tangle of fleece from a black Puma bag and gives it to Colette. They're similar in size, so the grey track pants and black hoodie with 'Superlovers' written in pink check across the back fit Colette fine.

"I guess this is better than my stinky slut clothes," says Colette. "But I can't believe I have to go out in public in track pants."

Colette works in the German Village, although she is not German. Her father is French, her mother is English, she grew up in Belgium. That seemed to be close enough and nobody has ever questioned her authenticity. After Johan broke up with her, she spent a week locked in her apartment in Antwerp, drinking cheap gin and scouring the Internet for jobs overseas. She wanted to be anywhere in the world, as far away as possible from her life, her teaching work, the city breathing memories of Johan. Colette considered nannying in the US and bartending on a cruise ship, but the theme park in Japan seemed to be what she needed. Something inside her called out to be something else, anything else, assume an alien identity. She needed to be in a foreign environment where nothing is familiar so she could recreate herself each day.

Usually she walks around inside the village, holding a basket of fake apples and smiling at children and old people. Today she walked around the front gate, handing out flyers for the wooden roller coaster as a string ensemble played Mozart. The German Village is loosely based on the Brothers Grimm stories. It's a replica of the village in Germany where the Brothers were born, and there's some other German stuff thrown in for good measure.

Colette actually didn't even know Snow White was German, or European for that matter. She has always associated Snow White with the image of the Disney character: short black hair, long dress with puffy sleeves. She didn't know, or had somehow forgotten, that Walt Disney's contrivance was based on a Brothers Grimm story.

After she gets dressed, Colette needs to go shopping. She starts to make her way to the station at the front entrance, a 25-minute walk away, to take the train two stops to the depato, *department store*. There's a sale at Hysteric Glamour right now, she thinks about the black vinyl pants she saw there on the weekend. Colette is making more money than she's ever made in her life, and she's discovered the joys of consuming. At home she only wore secondhand clothes, but since she's moved to Japan, she thinks nothing of spending hundreds of Euros on a shirt or pair of shoes.

On the walk to the station, the theme park feels as foreign as another planet. It's almost empty, with the occasional couple or family with small children strolling along the causeway, eating ice cream and deciding what country to go to next. There are no groups of school children. Colette had read in the monthly newsletter that the park is marketing itself to the schools as an opportunity for cross-cultural education. Public schools couldn't afford to travel to a foreign country, but a field trip to the gaikoku-mura is within their budgets.

On her way out of the European Village, Colette passes by only three people: a couple in designer clothes, a delivery person, and Johnny Ramone Guy, the shaggy-haired designer from the wax museum, holding a Styrofoam cup and onigiri in his hands. Even though he walked past her four times during her shift, taking a roller-coaster pamphlet each time, no glimmer of recognition registers in his face. She had read about Johnny Ramone Guy in the theme park newsletter, how his wax statues had been nominated for awards and his work is gaining international recognition.

Colette walks past the lake and the entrance to Treasure Island, set on a boat rather than an island. Some bored pirates hang around the ticket booth. The pirates are the wild children of the theme park's 300 employees, known to start food fights in the staff cafeteria and steal things from other pavilions. When Colette walks past, they whistle and shout, "Hey baby!" She doesn't look at them, avoiding the guitarist from The Long John Silvers, the punk rock band that regularly plays at staff appreciation night, whom she hit on a few weeks ago.

As she follows the shape of the Great Wall of China, Colette thinks about her latest Latin lover. She can hardly remember what he looks like, and she's slightly dreading the possibility of seeing him around the theme park or at staff appreciation night next week. The further she gets from the European Village, the more comfortable she feels, somehow protected by the plaster bricks of the Great Wall stacked beside her. This replica is a quarter of the height of the real Great Wall, and it stretches only about 750 metres, representing one tiny part of the wall.

The Great Wall ends just before the entrance to the Far East. Outside of Turkey, Colette is beckoned by a woman sitting at a small table. On a purple velvet cloth splattered with silver stars sits an illuminated crystal ball and a card that says "Fortune" in gold lettering, with a cluster of kanji characters below.

"I tell your fortune," the woman says in English with a Japanese accent. This surprises Colette. Wonder World is full of fortune-tellers, but this is the only one who has ever aggressively pursued Colette. Most of the theme park's clairvoyants sit demurely behind their little tables, filing their nails or discreetly dozing.

The sign reads 7500 yen. "No thanks," says Colette.

"I can read your palms or cards," says the woman, batting her long glued-on eyelashes, which make her look like she could actually be from some far eastern country.

"I don't have time," says Colette, turning away.

"You drink too much and you make sex with men you don't love." Colette stops. The woman points to a small folding chair and says gently, "Suwatte, kudasai." Colette sits down.

"My name is Kumiko. And you?"

"Colette." Saying her own name brings her back to the moment, makes her feel real, concrete.

"Co-ret-te. Where are you from?" She extends her palms, her long red nails inviting Colette's hands.

"Shouldn't you know that?" Kumiko only looks at her and rolls her eyes. "Belgium." Colette places her hands palms down in Kumiko's, feels warmth and a slight charge run across her skin.

"Why did you come to Japan?"

"To work here."

Kumiko runs her thumb across Colette's knuckles and Colette knows that this isn't just some woman in a fortune-teller costume.

"You leaving man in Be-lu-gi?"

"I didn't leave him, he.... Wait a minute."

Kumiko smiles, then closes her eyes and places the backs of Colette's hands on the purple velvet cloth. Her hands hover above Colette's and she mutters to herself in Japanese. Colette can understand only an exclamation of "Ii, na?" *Isn't that good?* Colette's hasn't studied Japanese at all since she started working at Wonder World, but she's picked up enough to identify the fortune-teller's strong Kansai accent. Her direct questions suggest she's from Osaka, rather than Kyoto or Kobe.

Kumiko wears a red, billowy shirt with flowing sleeves. Large silver hoops hang from her ears and big, jewelled rings adorn her fingers. Curls spring away from her head in all the right places, bouncing around when she moves. Most impressive about Kumiko is her exquisite make-up, which is perfectly flawless. Her lipstick is the exact red as her shirt and her skin is without lines or creases. It's difficult to tell her age, she seems old and young at the same time, well preserved, over 30 but younger than 60.

"Your hands covered in man," Kumiko finally says.

"Man? One man?"

"No," Kumiko laughs. "Many man. Belugi man, many dark-haired man. And there is another man. You don't know him. He looks you."

She closes her eyes and Colette wonders what she is invoking, what she is communicating with. The crystal ball sits between the two women, smooth and silent. It has to be just a prop, nobody actually uses these things, Colette thinks. The ball looks dense and solid, and Colette tries to imagine a halo of soft smoke circling the clear globe, lights swirling inside and scenes of her life rising to the surface.

Finally Kumiko says, "You are not moving. You stay in one place."

"What?"

"You are just going to circles. Around and around."

"What else do you see?"

"A donkey."

"A donkey? What does that mean?"

Kumiko shrugs. "This is just what your hands say. I only translate."

"What else do they say?"

Again she closes her eyes and guides her fingernails across the soft white skin of Colette's palms. "Here you are alone." Her hands come to a stop and Colette doesn't say anything.

"Is this true?" Kumiko asks.

"I don't need this right now," Colette says, gripping the edge of the table with both hands and pushing her chair back. She stands up, turns around and starts walking away.

"Hey!" yells the fortune-teller. "Hey! Okane! Okane!"

Colette drops two 1000-yen bills on the ground and picks up her pace, galloping away from the purple velvet table.

She has no idea where she is. Nothing looks familiar. Colette doesn't know the structure of the theme park, the logic with which the attractions are laid out, how the continents and geography reflect the world. Colette walks east and sort of north, ending up in Roshia, *Russia*. The controlled climate is a few degrees cooler than the rest of the theme park. The staff wears furry parkas, which look far too warm despite the cooler temperature.

Bloody fortune-teller, Colette says to herself. She looks at her betraying hands—the indecipherable codes across her palms, fingerprints containing a secret identity she can't unlock. Colette wonders what else her hands could tell her, if she were to bother asking; she curls her fingers into fists and walks faster, pushing deeper into Roshia.

In the middle of the cold vastness, Colette finds a carousel, lit up and shining like the North Star. The painted horses circle around and around, riding up and down the poles to a soundtrack of calliope music, a creepy carnivalesque "Twinkle Twinkle Little Star." Nobody rides any of the horses. Colette walks up to the attendant, who is reading a newspaper. He jumps when he sees her, stuffs the newspaper beside his chair. Colette flashes her Wonder World staff card, the attendant nods, and she pushes through the turnstile as the carousel pulls to a stop.

A black horse stops in front of Colette, red eyes flashing. The mane and tail look windswept, and the horse appears to be rearing. Colette puts her foot in the stirrup, climbs on, and the carousel starts to revolve again. The horses move in time to the music, up and down with the tempo. Colette looks at the horses around her, each one pink or yellow or baby blue with intricate illustrations on their hindquarters. She looks at the rump of the horse she sits on, and finds that it has no illustration. Just pure black, slight definition where there should be muscles.

The horse rides the pole, synchronized with the motion of the horses around it. When her horse is low, Colette can only see the sides of the horses around her, but after rising up the pole, she can see over their heads, out past the fence around the carousel. The horse passes replicas of Russian landmarks and architecture, and the attendant in his seat has resumed reading his newspaper.

In the distance she sees the Eiffel Tower, rising up from beside the German Village. She has no idea how to get there, or how she got where she is. The carousel continues its circles and Colette wonders how many times it will go around. She remembers when she got separated from her parents at the Space Mountain ride at Paris Disneyland when she was six years old. At the beginning of the line, her parents pushed through the turnstiles, smiling and waving at her as they stepped onto the ride. The turnstile came up to her eye level;

she tried to slide under it, but her older sister held her hand and prevented her from following.

"Twinkle twinkle little star," Colette sings along with the music, which also picks up pace. "How I wonder what you are. Up above the world so high, like a diamond in the sky." It's been a long time since she saw the stars, which are obscured by Japan's lit-up urban centres. The carousel starts to pick up speed; Colette reaches for the reins but there aren't any. She wraps her arms around the steed, slides her fingers across cold smoothness, and holds on to the horse with everything in her. The carousel feels like it's going to spin right off its axis, launch into space, the horses around her also gaining speed. She feels like she's gotten caught in a race, but nobody seems to be winning, they just keep spinning faster and faster, like a discus flying and spiraling.

The music accelerates and increases in pitch. Colette digs her feet into the stirrups and grips the horse's neck. The carousel whirs past the attendant reading his paper, past the Kremlin and the giant mammoth, the statue of Dostoyevsky. She imagines the carousel snapping off its axis and rocketing like a flashing marquis sign across the bright blue sky, soaring over entire continents. All she can do is keep herself from sliding off the horse's smooth fiberglass back and hold on for the ride.

Between Stops

Kyoto Station

The last train out of the city pulls away from the platform and I am thrown against the man next to me. He nods, continues reading his newspaper. Businessmen surround me, wearing rumpled suits and holding briefcases, on their way home from obligatory drinks with the coworkers on a Friday night. They struggle to hold themselves up, clutch the rings with both hands. The smell of alcohol and cigarettes wafts through the air. A man is sitting on the bench seat in front of me, holding a can of beer, his head tipped to one side, mouth open. The woman next to him leans to her right, clutches her Louis Vuitton purse. A high school student stands beside the door, still in uniform although school finished nine hours ago. She silently keys an e-mail message into her cell phone, her 'loose socks' bunched around her ankles like legwarmers.

Half of the people in this car hold cell phones, engaged in silent e-mail conversations. I am the only foreigner, and so far nobody has tried to practice their English on me. I look out the window, past the people around me, avoiding my own reflection.

Pachinko parlours, karaoke bars and bright convenience store signs whiz by. I start to feel dizzy. I don't know what it is, the smell of liquor everywhere or the flashing neon outside the window. I focus on a ferris wheel in the distance.

Toji

I have spent too much time on these trains, can recognize the station by the length of the platform, the sound of brakes scraping. Eight months ago, when I first arrived, everything was a mystery, each stop an unexplored possibility. But I know this stop is not so different from the one before or the one after it. The platform is grey concrete; there are some benches, some standing ashtrays, a vending machine full of coffee and energy drinks. Through the turnstiles and outside the station is a myriad of noodle restaurants, sushi bars, fast food joints.

I ride these trains to work everyday, like all the people around me. I am Anne of Green Gables. I lead groups of schoolchildren through Wonder World's Canada pavilion, recite a memorized speech about the Rocky Mountains and Niagara Falls, sell tickets for the log ride. I answer questions about skiing and Canadian holidays and beavers.

Today I went straight from work to a bar called Usagi, *rabbit*, and spent the evening drinking sake and talking to the master, a lovely man named Daisuke who wears his guitar strapped across his chest while he makes drinks. I managed to have a three-hour conversation in a language that's not my own about Japanese food, Canadian food, food of the world. Yes we have sushi in Canada, no we don't eat maple syrup with every meal, I like Japanese food more than British food.

I am still wearing my Anne wig, long red braids hanging down my back. I feel them swing with the motion of the train. Daisuke loves the wig. He loves Anne of Green Gables. We listened to the Rolling Stones and he told me about his trip to Canada three years ago, how he drove a rented car from Vancouver to the Rockies, how he loved the town of Golden.

Momoyamagoryomae

The train tracks are lined with single-room apartments. Fluorescent lights flicker in some, TVs flash in others, brief glimpses of people living their lives. The trains must send shudders through the buildings. Past another row of

28

pachinko parlours and karaoke bars is a massive apartment complex, similar to the one I live in. The windows of the five buildings face the other direction, all I can see are five grids of entrance lights.

The train shifts tracks without warning and the sleeping, still standing businessman leans into me. I stumble into the woman next to me, she braces herself on the guy next to her. What am I doing here? I mean here on the last train, struggling for balance, I mean the muffled giggles of drunk college boys and the snoring businessmen around me. I hold onto the ring and focus on the outline of a three-storey pagoda temple against the haze of the city.

Giggles and whispers behind me. I turn around, I shouldn't do it but I do. OLs. Office Ladies, another Japanese appropriation of English. Two of them, they hold their hands to their mouths, as if trying to hide their laughter.

"Kawaii!!" they giggle in unison, pointing at my head.

I shrug and say "Wakarahen." *I don't understand*, in the Kyoto dialect. I'm not in the mood. It's been a long day and I'm sick of Japanese.

The OLs are so cute and stylish, in their Chanel sweaters, their dainty feet squeezed into pointy high heels. They hold Gucci purses and wear a lot of make-up. They are drunk and clutching each other, swaying with the motion of the train. Bumping into, and held up by, the people around them. I feel like an ogre woman next to these ladies of the office. I feel large and vulgar in my running shoes and Anne dress, the stupid ruffled and puffy smock thing I'm forced to wear everyday.

One of them leans over and tugs my right braid. I feel the wig slide. "Hair...real?" she blurts out, her friend giggling and applauding her English. The train pulls to a stop, the doors open, and the ladies are swept onto the platform, waving, shouting their e-mail addresses at me.

Ogura

This is where the city ends and the suburbs begin. The intercom crackles and a man's voice says: "Sumimasen, konbonwa. Tsugi wa..." garble garble garble. I have no idea what he's saying, it doesn't sound like English or Japanese, all feedback and fuzz. The businessman next to me automatically opens his eyes, shuffles through the open door. Several other people walk off. Nobody gets on. The driver leans his head out the window, blows a whistle held between white-gloved fingers. The train pulls away and I stumble again.

No-one at home knows that I am Anne of Green Gables. I've told them, instead, that I host a game show and for some reason they believe this. When they ask for copies of the show, I tell them that there is nothing as archaic as VHS videos in Japan, people watch TV on their cell phones and e-mail their favourite shows to friends. My original purpose for coming here was an internship with an NGO. My position was cut three weeks after my arrival, and the Anne of Green Gables gig fell into my lap. My only options at the time were to be Anne or teach English or go home. I don't remember why I opted for Anne.

The scenery changes from narrow streets and cramped apartments to rows of identical grey homes and rice fields. I can see only large spaces of darkness where the rice fields are, perfect lines of street lights, a 7-Eleven sign rising into the night.

Iseda

The high school student gets off and the train pauses at the platform to let a rapid express train go by. It passes with a rumble, the windows shake in their frames, I tighten my grip on the ring.

I have had earthquake anxieties since I came to this country. I can detect the earth's slightest rearrangement under my feet. There have been three quakes so far. The first happened while I sat in the staff cafeteria at work, drinking coffee with Zeus and Paul Bunyan. The building swayed, people screamed, I was the only person who crawled under a table. The next happened while I was drinking sake and playing poker at a friend's house. Only a tremor, but we instantly sobered up. The most recent quake was while I lay on my futon watching TV. Again, the swaying sensation, I imagined my floor crashing into the apartment beneath me. I instinctively jumped out of bed and stood in a doorway. That was when I realized nothing has any support, it could all fall at any moment.

I have since prepared an 'earthquake emergency kit': some instant ramen, candles, bottled water, Japanese-English dictionary in a gym bag next to my washing machine. It'll be no help if I'm at work, out with friends, riding the train when the big one hits. But I sleep better at night.

Mukaijima

My stop. With both hands I grip the rings and resist being pulled along with the stream moving out the door. Unable to hold myself up, I slide onto the green velour bench seat in front of me. Only three people remain in the car: myself, a sleeping college student and a girl with headphones on. The whistle blows, the doors close and I imagine the city at the end of this train line, shining and glistening in the night. I imagine a sprawling maze of lights and darkness. I will lose myself there, wait for dawn.

I look at the advertisements that line the walls, hang from the ceiling. They look brilliant, as if they are lit from within, as if this is the first time I've seen them. These ads are an indecipherable code to me. Not simply another language, but three, possibly four other languages. A woman in a kimono stands next to a steaming hot spring, holding an iron in her hands. Four eggs with legs and arms wear little baseball caps. A man dressed like a Viking, the words 'NO LOAN' above his head.

I look at myself in the window across from me. One braid hangs over my shoulder, my head looks lop-sided. I don't adjust the wig. Beyond my reflection is a line of pachinko parlours and karaoke bars, neon signs flashing a Morse code into the night air. A rescue message, perhaps a warning.

PART 2: USAGI

Daisuke wears his guitar at work so he can practice when business is slow. It's Friday night, seven o'clock. He usually doesn't open this early, but I e-mailed his cell phone when I got off work and told him to meet me here. He rushed down only because he knew I'd be wearing the wig. I am the only customer, and will be until people show up after So-on-ji finishes playing at the 'livehouse' down the street.

He makes a couple of rum and cokes and says, "I want you to listen my favourite record of all time." He puts on David Bowie, silently strums along with the opening bars of Ziggy Stardust.

The wall next to the bar is lined with shelves of records. Records, records and more records, I couldn't even count how many. They are alphabetical and sort of chronological. They are all rock and nothing but rock. No techno, no jazz, no country (except a little Patsy Cline), no hip hop, no blues (other than two Howlin' Wolf albums).

The place is small. It's dark, too, the only light coming from two hanging bulbs, a lava lamp and a string of white Christmas lights twisted along the bar. Records occupy one whole wall. I am sitting on one of the chrome stools at the bar, and behind me are two wooden tables with long bench seats. It's cozy and woodsy in here, making me feel like I'm in a cabin or ski lodge. The walls are plastered with Led Zeppelin posters and vintage American concert flyers. The back of the door is a collage of photos: Daisuke performing with his band; Daisuke fishing with friends on Lake Biwa; Daisuke boarding a Greyhound bus in Calgary.

I discovered Usagi by accident a few months ago. I was exploring the back alleys of Kyoto when I saw the checkered door squeezed between hostess bars and ramen shops. The name of the bar was indicated on a signboard with a hand-painted Beavis and Butthead cartoon, Beavis saying, "Let's party!" and Butthead responding, "Yeah! We don't give the fuck!" I went inside and was surprised to find an English-speaking bartender who proudly informed me that he had spent hours painting the cartoon characters himself. He introduced himself as Daisuke, then insisted I call him 'Brian.' "Like Brian Wilson," he said. "He is genius. And Bryan Adams. He is not genius, but he is Canadian."

I'm suppressing the urge to woo Daisuke. There's nothing I want to do more than convince him to fall in love with me. I'm so crazy about his mullet, the tight black jeans he always wears, his cute broken English. And the guitar, of course. But I'm holding myself back. I'm giving myself time, don't want to rush anything.

"Listen to the new song I write," he says, gently lifting the needle off the record. He strums a discordant melody, croons "whoa baby, oooh yeah, baby." It sounds like metal strings slapping against wood.

"That's the most beautiful thing I've ever heard," I tell him.

Daisuke bows his head, sings "Arigato gozaimasu," and plays the rest of the song for me.

Daisuke has told me bits about his life, and I have tried to piece these details together into some kind of coherent whole. I know he studied business in Tokyo after graduating from high school. He had no interest in business, but his university entrance exam scores determined his major. After finishing his degree, he went to London to study English as a Second Language. He dropped out of school, squatted in north London, and worked in pubs. Somehow, he ended up directing music videos. He says some words with a slight British accent, for which he credits Robert Plant rather than life in England.

I'm not sure how long he lived in London. Or even how old he is now. His stories have no dates or lengths of time, he tells me only random, loosely connected events. After London, he came back to Japan. He travelled around Southeast Asia, North America, he lived in Los Angeles and worked as some kind of designer. He also mentioned living with a woman, an artist/musician he described as "a white Yoko Ono." When I asked Daisuke why he came back to Japan, to run a small rock bar and play guitar in a band, he placed his hand on his heart and replied, "Here is my home."

Daisuke makes me another rum and coke, but he has hardly even touched his. He's just started working, has a long night ahead of him. "Are you wasting tonight?" he asks.

"'Getting wasted,'" I correct him. "No, I don't think so."

I've been on one date since I came to this country. I met Shuhei, who runs the Amazon Jungle Safari ride at work, in line at the cafeteria and we started up a cell phone e-mail flirtation. I charmed him with a series of haiku about the theme park, and he asked me out for dinner. We ate at a prison-themed restaurant, sat in a tiny jail cell bound to our chairs with handcuffs. After dinner, we walked through Gion to Yasaka shrine and watched cherry blossom festival revelry. I haven't heard from him since. I see him occasionally at work, not too often because we work on different continents. He is nervous and jittery when we do talk, flinches as if he expects me to hit him.

"When are you going back to Canada?" Daisuke asks me in Japanese, tuning the guitar.

"I don't know. Not for a while, I guess. I have another four months until I finish my contract."

"You won't get homesick. You are around Canada things every day. You are lucky to work in a place that's just like Canada."

"Yeah, sure," I say, handing him my empty glass for a refill. I think about all the Canada things I see every day: the airbrushed mural of the Rocky Mountains, the miniature illuminated Niagara Falls, the massive stuffed beaver who welcomes guests with a squeaky robotic "Konnichiwa!!!" Totally just like Canada.

My most recent obsession is a man known only as Crazy Life, so called because of the cryptic 'Crazy Life Kar Klub' T-shirt he always wears to the gym. He caught my eye with the rhinestone 'Crazy Life' pendant he wears around his neck. I see him at the gym every Wednesday night, and it's come to be the highlight of my week. Crazy Life is a hunk of manly manliness, much more buff and built than the average Japanese male. We talk every week, banal conversations about the weather or TV, which I memorize and recreate for my co-workers. He brought me a picture of his Crazy Life-mobile, some kind of 'hopping' van, with flashing lights and wings and tinted windows. Last Wednesday, I worked up the nerve to ask him out for drinks, but he didn't show up at the gym.

I started going to the gym when I felt like I was going to bust out of my Anne dress, when I felt the zipper straining to hold it all together. I couldn't understand why this was happening, since I live on convenience store sushi and canned coffee. I joined the Joyous Healthy Club because I couldn't stand the idea of telling my 90-pound supervisor, who eats Calorie-Mate food bars for three meals a day, who has a six-inch waist and no hips or thighs, that I need a new dress.

"No more rum for you," Daisuke says, taking my glass. He puts a ceramic sake cup, no bigger than a shot glass, in front of me. "You must try this. It's awamori, from Okinawa and it's very special. This cost more than 20,000 yen." That's roughly 200 Canadian dollars. He pulls a bottle from under the bar and fills the sake cup. Curled up in the bottom of the bottle is a snake.

"Jesus Christ, Daisuke." He gives me a mock-stern look. "I mean Brian. Jesus Christ, Brian. What the hell is that?"

"The snake's poison makes it power." I tip my head back and shoot the poison-infused elixir. "Oishi, ne?" *Delicious, isn't it.* I nod. My nose is burning, my throat feels numb, the hairs on the back of my neck curl. He pours me another.

At eleven o'clock, the bar fills with people from the 'live-house'. They are drunk and rowdy, tell us about So-on-ji's amazing performance. Their voices and drinking games sound like they're coming from far away. I let my head fall to the bar because I can't hold it up any longer.

"I need to go home," I slur to Daisuke.

"It's getting late. You better hurry to the train station." He leans across the bar, tips the wig back from my forehead, then laughs. "You are wasting!" This time I don't correct him.

I slide off the stool, balance myself on the bar. It's a good thing I'm leaving before I do anything stupid. I am yearning to touch his hair, craving a kiss before I walk out the door. Instead, he strikes his guitar and calls out "Kiyotsukete, ne!" *Take care.* I step into the fresh air, hope I sober up a bit on the walk to the train station.

PART 3: END OF THE LINE

I am awakened by a train attendant tapping my arm. "Sumimasen," he says, bowing. He nudges awake a man sleeping on a bench seat across from me, urges him out the door. The man stumbles along the platform toward the escalator. I have passed out on the train and awakened in the heart of the city. In the dead centre. I get up and walk off the train, with a few other groggy-looking people. The escalators have stopped working for the night, so I walk up the down staircase, beginning my ascension to the surface of the earth.

There is no train back to where I came from, I am stuck here until morning. Five hours until the first train, I will have to find a way to amuse myself in central Osaka. I push my way through the turnstiles, leaving the train station behind me.

Outside the turnstiles is a long underground tunnel. I have been here before, I know the passages I must go through, the escalators I must ride up before I am at street level again. I have walked past these restaurants with displays of plastic food in the windows, these closed clothing stores and bookstores and juice bars. This place is like a mall, except it's not, it's underground, it's part of the station. This is the city under the city, ghostly and subterranean.

I catch a glimpse of my reflection in the window of a sock store. My dress, my Anne wig, I am fully intact. I can't see my face, but I can imagine the dark circles under my eyes, my puffy lips, my smeared mascara.

I come to a sort of intersection. A sign hangs from the ceiling, yellow letters on a black background. To my right are Exits 1-5, to my left are Exits 9-13, straight ahead are Exits 16-21. None of this means anything to me, these exits, these numbers. Usually, when I come to this city, I go straight to Exit 8, which isn't even indicated here and which I don't even know how to get to. But usually I go to Exit 8 and I ride the escalator to street level, to my favourite shopping mall and restaurants.

I feel a panic attack coming on. I imagine the morning janitor finding my unconscious body in a heap on the floor, beneath the sign. I take a deep breath and walk straight. I will go out the first exit I see. It's starting to get late and I need another drink.

37

Exit 9 is a long corridor at the top of the escalator. I walk toward the end. I see a dark narrow stairwell; beside it is a thick black door. I choose the door, I choose the darkness over the stairs. I don't know what it is, the blackness or the pulsing throb of beats coming from behind the door. But I choose the door.

Before I can pull it open, a skinny shirtless guy in black vinyl pants pushes out and heads toward the stairs. I slip in as he leaves and find the entrance to a club. Some kind of goth club, black clothes and make-up everywhere. A woman with long black hair and a bandage over one eye sits behind a small table. I feel her eye assessing my puffy dress and long red wig. I hand her 2000 yen for the admission fee and she stamps a skull and crossbones on the back of my hand. I push through the door into the main room.

Goths are scary creatures. Morbid, dark, macabre, their black fashion reflecting their black outlook on the world. I remember there were a few goths at my high school. I didn't have much to do with them. I aligned myself with the hippies and skateboarders rather than the kids in black who sat in the back of the classroom, the kids who walked down the halls like a thick sea of death, a united front of evil. I always found them intimidating, depressing, and just weird.

There are some of those here, women in long black dresses, guys with white face paint. There is lots of vinyl and leather and blackness. But there is another strain of goth culture, one that can be unique only to Japan. 'Lolita Goths,' girls who dress more like Little Bo Peep than Siouxie Sioux. I have seen these girls before, in magazines, hanging out in downtown Tokyo and Osaka, but I have never seen them up close.

I head straight for the bar and order a double gin and tonic. I stand against the back wall and take it all in. The cute goth girls in their frilly and puffy frocks. The more traditional long-haired goths in draping layers of black lace and satin. Skinny guys in vinyl and white face paint. One girl, in a pink Bo Peep dress and striped stockings, holds a red, fluffy devil doll. The drink feels cool and sharp as it slides down my throat. It's about time. I sobered up a bit on the train and feel a hangover coming on. I finish it in a few big gulps and make my way back to the bar for another.

As I'm returning to my spot, a boy grabs me by the arm. He is shouting something in Japanese and waving around a tiny digital camera. I can't hear anything he says over the pounding industrial, and I indicate this by pointing at my ears and shaking my head. He holds up his camera again, and points back and forth between us. I get it. Together. He wants to take a picture of the two of us together. He in his PVC, me in my Anne dress.

He gives his friend the camera and poses with me, then they exchange places. I flash a 'peace' sign. They say something to me in Japanese, but I can't hear them, so I nod and pretend I know what they're talking about. I do this a lot, and not only when I'm in loud nightclubs.

I down two more gin and tonics and hit the dance floor. What happens next is blurry, pixelated, like a flashing strobe light. I dance with some Bo Peep goths, they tell me they are seventeen and live in the countryside three hours away by train. Everybody clears the floor for an S/M performance. A woman with a whip lashes a silver-haired girl, the crowd cheers her on. I meet some foreigner guys filming girls making out in the bathroom; they claim they are making a promotional film for the club.

I encounter the boys with the camera again. They pet my hair, cooing and giggling. One of them asks me a question, I can't hear what he says so I smile and nod. He carefully removes the wig from my head and places it on his own. His friend and I jump up and down, laughing and pointing. His friend pulls out the camera and takes a picture, then they trade places. People come over, friends, the girl from the door, put on the wig and pose for mug shots. Spots from the repeated camera flash swim in front of my eyes. I watch the wig being passed from hand to hand, crowd surfing above the dance floor.

I push my way out the doors, back into the corridor and up the stairs to Exit 9. I am craving fresh air. The street is full of people making their way to wherever they're going. In front of me is the entrance to Babylon, a tall building full of bars, which my co-workers and I call a 'tower of bars.' A directory lists some of the contents of Babylon: Bar Indies 4 fl, Pica Pica 3 fl, Skydive 6 fl, Heaven 9 fl, Rock Bar 7 fl.

I climb the stairs to Happy Karaoke on the fifth floor. The guy at the front counter doesn't say anything as I walk past him and down the hallway lined with frosted glass doors. Badly sung J-pop hits and enka classics fill the hall.

A man steps out of the bathroom and sees me standing in the hallway. "Oh, pretty girl!" he says. "Pretty hair!" I nod, not really in agreement, more of a greeting. He opens the door to his karaoke box and beckons me to follow him. I step into the tiny room he and his friends have rented by the hour.

"I am Takada," he says. "These are my friends. What is your name?" He speaks as if he is chewing on a hard candy, or toffee. Trying to remember the order of English words, their shapes foreign in his mouth.

"Anne," I answer.

"Nice to meet you." He speaks seriously, with intent, and hands me a glass of beer. He points at a guy across the room, who sings along with the words on the screen and claps his hands. "He is Matsuda. Today is his birthday."

He calls out for his friends' attention and introduces me. They greet me with a unanimous "Hooiy!!" The guy who I met in the hallway is in his mid to late thirties and he's wearing jeans and a T-shirt. He's with six friends, all men, all around the same age, all dressed differently. Some are dressed in white shirts and suits, as if they went out straight from work, others are more casual. They seem to have known each other for a long time, like friends from university or something.

"Anne-san, sing a song," says the birthday boy, passing me the remote and a thick book of song listings. Mostly Japanese songs, of course, but there is a small section of English classic rock and top-40 songs in the back. I scan the pages until I find the substantial B section. I press 9-5-4-3-7 into the remote and wait for my selection to flash across the monitor.

This is how the karaoke box works: you rent a room by the hour and the price may or may not include drinks and food. When you want to sing a song, you press the code into the remote control and within a few minutes, depending on how many other selections there are, the tune will play and the lyrics will come up on the monitor screen. There are two or three mics in the room and anybody can sing. The room is set up almost like a living-room, with couches and a low table. Sometimes there's a stage, sometimes there isn't. There's a phone on the wall, and you can call down to the front desk and order drinks or food whenever you want.

The guy with the mic finishes off his mournful old ballad, another guy sings a girly pop song, and then my selection pops up on the screen. I take the mic as the opening piano bars fill the room.

"When I find myself in times of trouble, Mother Mary comes to me," I sing. The men sit up in their seats, mouth the lyrics. "Singing words of wisdom, let it be, let it be."

Takada picks up another mic and chimes in with "Though the nights are cold and lonely, there's still a light that shines on me." Everybody in Japan knows all the words to all the Beatles' songs. The rest of the guys stand up and join in. I pass off my mic to one of the suits, grab a lighter from the table and hold it in the air, everybody follows the motion of the flame. Soon we all have our arms around one another, singing along to "Let It Be."

I push up the last flight of stairs and walk down a long corridor lined with secretive doors that lead to closet-sized bars. At the end of the corridor hangs a cloth with the hiragana character yu—*hot water*. A sento, *public bath*. I take off my shoes at the door and put them in a little shoe locker, locking it with a little wooden key.

I hand 350 yen to the old man behind the counter and walk to the women's change-room. Japanese public baths don't have the same negative connotations as public baths in North America. They are simply places to bathe, to become clean again. A TV is set up on the dividing wall between the men's and women's side, so both genders can watch. An old samurai drama plays on the screen. I open a locker, undo the zipper at the back of my grime-coated dress and peel it away from my skin. I put it in the locker and take off my bra, underwear and socks. I take off the wig and look at myself in the mirror. My short hair is matted against my skull. My make-up has run and I have black circles around my eyes. I look like hell.

On the wall above the mirror is a poster of Brad Pitt. He is wearing a suit and posing with a can of Roots coffee. I live for canned coffee. And I live for Brad Pitt's advertising campaign with Roots canned coffee. My favourite TV commercial is where Brad, playing a disgruntled office worker, drinks a can of coffee and pushes a photocopier down a flight of stairs. I know the feeling.

I open a sliding door and step into the room with the baths. There's nobody else here, I have the whole place to myself. I walk across the tiled floor to the row of low showers against the back wall and sit down on a little plastic stool. I fill a bucket with water and pour it over my head, feel the hot water cascade down my neck and my back. Rivers of black run down my legs. I squirt a handful of soap from the dispenser and rub my hands together. Thick foamy suds flow from between my fingers. I rub the suds over my body and scrub and scrub, until there are red streaks across my skin. I feel dirt and dead skin cells and city grime squeeze out of my pores. I want to scrub until the top layer of skin comes off, until all that remains is tender baby pink skin.

I turn on the shower head and rinse myself off, until the last trace of soap and grime washes down the drain. There are six tubs in here: cold, herbal, jacuzzi, electric, and two normal tubs.

I walk over to the electric tub and stand at the edge, looking in. An invisible current vibrates across the surface of the water. The electric tub seems like it should be dangerous. I've never been able to get into one before, turned off by the idea of electric-charged water. I dip my foot through the electric current and into the water. There's no flash, no bolt of electricity, no shock. I feel only a small muscle spasm, my foot jerks away from me. I submerge the rest of my leg, and my other leg, and slowly lower myself into the tub, feeling the spasms move up my body. It doesn't hurt or tingle, but all my muscles feel as if I'm clenching them. I wonder about the possibility of a heart attack or something.

The electric tub begins to freak me out, so I move to the jacuzzi tub. I sit down until only my head is above water. The jets send a pulsing surge into my back and my thighs, like a massage. I take a deep breath and pull my head under, feel bubbles scurry across my face. I count to ten, then twenty—the water is scalding—I keep counting until I reach 106, then I break through the surface and inhale. The air rushes into my lungs.

I lean against the smooth tiles and sit in the tub until my toes wrinkle, until I feel soaked all the way through. Only a thin wall separates the women's tubs from the men's tubs. I can hear three or four loud animated voices discussing something on the other side. Probably yakuza, Japanese gangsters. Who else would be using the public baths at five in the morning?

I re-enter the change-room and buy a little towel from a vending machine, dry myself off. Next to the vending machine is a stack of clean and folded yukata, cotton robes, available for rent for 500 yen. I take one from the top of the stack and tie it around my waist. It is a soft blue, feels like it's been washed and dried many times.

I take my Anne dress out of the locker and put it in the garbage. I take the wig out and replace the key for the locker. I walk out of the change-room, past the guy at the counter, and put my shoes on in the entrance way. I walk down the hallway to a final flight of stairs, a chain link gate across them, marked with a sign. I can't read the sign, but I can assume it says something like 'Danger, don't come in here.' I push the gate, it opens without resistance. I walk up the stairs and come to the roof. There's no other place I could go.

I can see most of the city from here, rooftops and power lines stretching out to the suburbs and eventually the ocean. The sun is starting to rise, casting a soft pink glow over everything. A cluster of skyscrapers erupting from the business district catches the morning light. Toward the west it is still night, a few stars sparkle above the horizon. An airplane, taking off from Kansai Airport, leaves a scar across the sky.

I'm still holding the Anne wig. It feels soft and limp in my hands, like a dead rabbit. Strands of hair have come loose, stick out everywhere. I sit down and dangle my legs over the edge of the building. From here, the city looks clean and peaceful, the neon muted, the dirt and grime obscured.

I imagine layers of train tracks twisting beneath the streets, a whole other city below this city. The trains have started running by now, it's almost time to make my way home. Make my way to my little apartment between two cities. To my single room, tiny balcony, my futon, TV, book-shelf.

I hold the wig up, try to smooth the escaped hairs. It's covered in dirt from strangers' hands, smoke and alcohol from the dance floor and karaoke bar. I'm glad that it's not my own hair, that I can hold it between two fingers, from the top of the crown. The braids hang even. I pull my fingers apart and let it fall. It tumbles over itself, an acrobatic dance through the air, to the pavement below. It lands next to a mailbox, the braids stuck out at awkward angles, like broken legs. I pull my yukata tight around me, re-tie it, and start the descent to the station below, to the train ride home.

LARRY BROWN

Pin Girl

"Are you alone?"

"Let me turn down the radio."

Jack sticks the phone to his chest. The curtains are drawn but sunlight cuts the wall. On the television a man holds up a frying pan and people applaud. Jack motions to the girl. She glides to the far end of the couch, taking the remote with her. He grabs for it, straining the phone cord, but with her bare foot she fends him off, blocking, swatting his hand, smiling to the television. She is the most flexible person he has ever met.

"There," he tells his mother.

"You're like me, we like our radio. I don't understand the hoopla over these computers."

"How's the hip? Your hip."

"My hip was a month ago."

"Hips are like that."

"But so," and then she does it, patters out one of her dry coughs. "I thought I should be the one to tell you this."

"This time of day, you almost didn't catch me in."

"Next, I'm afraid you won't answer when I call."

"I'm fine," says Jack.

His mother talks. Jack flicks the phone cord with his finger. He tastes peanut butter.

He interrupts. "How do you know for sure he has?"

"Because I didn't get up this morning intending to make something like this up. That's a horrible attitude, fixing it in your head that no-one other than you speaks before thinking."

Jack gathers the crumbs on the coffee table, brushes them to the floor.

"Neither of us, your father included, wants it coming to this. Your father will admit that himself. Blame is not our style, we're beyond that."

Jack says, "I wish they'd make a cordless phone that does not need a battery. They invent everything else."

"Jack?"

"Somebody should figure it out, they'd get rich."

"Jack, will you go over there?"

Jack's reply comes easier than he believes it should. He is not surprised.

"But be firm," says his mother.

After Jack hangs up, the girl changes the channel. The remote is pinched between her feet. She eats a pretzel.

"Never mind," says Jack, getting up.

The driveway to the house is empty. Jack parks across the street, goes up onto the side verandah and knocks at the aluminum door anyway. It is locked.

He opens one of the lawn chairs folded against the wall, for no reason he positions the chair so he can see the front end of his car. He sits, reaches out his foot to tag the spindle railing. The driveway has an oil stain. He can say he waited.

Jack starts in the chair. The haze lingers. He has been dozing.

In the driveway his father stands at a car door.

"Set another spot for supper," he says, loudly.

Jack curses himself.

"Dar," says his father, "it's Jack. Jack's here and made himself right at home."

At the driver's side Darlene shields her face from the sun, she wears a wide-brimmed hat. Her gold slacks and blouse shimmer. She flattens a dandelion with her cane, grinds it into the ground.

"That's you across the street," his father behind the car now, with a shovel, "that's you advertising your arrival on the scene."

"Got those chairs on sale," another skimming step brings Darlene to the railing up to the verandah, "end of the season last year. But go in the early part of any season and there are

49

the crowds, buying precisely when the stores would have them buy, taking on the full sticker price, making a smorgasbord of excuses. That's how inflation works, it's mostly voluntary."

"A shovel isn't a rake, Dar."

"Wait till the sale tags of November."

"Not shovels."

"My, it's a lovely day. We have too few."

"This is a first-rate purchase, it's smart and fair. Fair is not always cheap,"

Jack folds up the lawn chair, his head clearing.

"I went prepared to be like everyone else and spend more than I should," says Darlene. "That is what's different in this case."

"It's settled then." Jack's father bites an end of his moustache. His face is stubbly grey and the sleeveless sweatshirt he has on barely reaches his waist.

"What did Susie tell you?" says Darlene.

"I don't know," says Jack.

Darlene speaks to a place beside him, "She's not about to invite someone who's a stranger to her into the house and offer the deluxe tour. She's practical, and I don't mean cautious." Darlene hooks her cane over the railing at the back of the verandah.

"Aloha, stranger." His father grips him by the arm and Jack does what he can to not react. He has inches on his father.

"I can't stay till supper."

"Suit yourself."

Jack clamps a hand down onto his father's shoulder. "Maybe I can."

"Maybe you will."

They hold onto one another. His father's moustache is fuller than the last time Jack saw him, bushes over his lip.

"Roger, I've changed my mind and decided. We'll put it there, where the fence can help frame it. If I have to trek into the yard anytime I want to enjoy the garden, I'm going to enjoy it that much less. As for you, Jack," says Darlene, "I'm curious."

To Jack, neither of them feels to be the first to let go. They haven't, and then, his father's stubbly face retreating, they have. Jack resists the urge to look at his arm. He can't leave without collecting his father.

"Are you a gardener? Can that be listed as a hobby of yours?" The wrinkles in the back of Darlene's shiny blouse seem to move on their own. "I'm going on a hunch, and if it's a whim, why, no-one's keeping score. Roger hasn't spilled any beans. I'm not asking you to repeat what I already know so we can claim we chitchatted when it was nothing of the sort. And, Roger, do let him speak."

"Why wouldn't I?"

"Thank you."

"Me?" says Jack.

Then Darlene calls, "Hello, Bruce," and waves.

In the next yard a man with an armful of brush turns in the wrong direction.

Jack says to his father, "The thing you did with old tinfoil, you made a ball. It got pretty big."

"That's not a hobby."

"It was a lot of tinfoil. Where'd so much come from?"

"She needs an answer from you."

"Let me see. My answer is, I garden all I want to."

"Now that wasn't too difficult, was it. We can label it my hunch then."

"That's our Dar." Jack's father leans on the shovel, the waistband of his boxer shorts appearing where the sweatshirt rides up. He looks tired.

"Do you have a question for me, Jack, since I already went and did it to you? Rather boldly, I might add."

"Hello all right," calls the man in the next yard.

Yet when no-one mentions it Jack figures he must be in on it alone: the large woman stands at the aluminum door, inside a faint reflection of the verandah that includes Jack and his leaning father. She mouths something to him, her eyes narrowing.

"Who's Susie?" says Jack.

Then Darlene says, "There's Susie."

"We need to do exactly nothing here for a while."

Jack is thirsty.

"I don't have to explain why to you."

"Don't."

"You going to leave the engine running?"

Susie reclines her seat. There is only one notch further to go but she continues jerking the handle and pushing back, sighing. Jack feels his seat tremor.

"I'm going to leave the engine running," he says.

But soon he wonders if she has fallen asleep. He is supposed to be taking her to the train station so she can exchange her ticket for one back to Kingston tomorrow. But here they are, pulled over, also just as she asked. Jack has time. How much of his time does this woman think she can take up?

A cape and silk scarves and long billowy dress. He smells felt. He didn't realize he knew how felt smells or even that felt had a smell yet there it is. A smooth, quiet smell.

"I've forgotten your name," says Susie, eyes closed.

After a moment Jack tells her.

"When I don't hear my name, Jack, I don't forget what I didn't hear."

Pink, Jack has heard, or read, begins returning to lungs the day smoking is quit, and he doesn't smoke but the idea of a returning pink is stubborn and appealing and nearly promising enough to start though he would rather the actual sick stinky smoking part not have to be involved but he does like the idea of pink. That pink is something. He has his doubts about it.

"Americans," he says, "I hate them."

He swipes at dust.

"Ask anybody the same thing, there's not a speck out of place in that whole question. Americans, yes or no?"

A layer of dust coats the dashboard.

"I mean, is Heaven run by a bunch of flipping monkeys?"

His arms are conducting.

"Let me screw this into my head. Detroit. Detroit, as in midwest. That's what they call it, the midwest, there'll be highway signs and a Baptist marching band, so then are they trying to tell me Windsor is the midwest? It's right across the bridge. *Windsor?* Midwest my heinie, at Detroit and Windsor things have hardly gotten going but look, the Americans are pretending they're already way out in front."

When he turns, her eyes are still closed.

"Americans. They deserve whatever they get."

Susie opens her eyes and her door. "I need a treat. You'll wait?"

"There won't be a single honest cowboy hat in all of Detroit. That's what I'm talking about."

The smell of felt fades from the car.

Susie fans herself, hair wisping. For her treat from the convenience store Jack expected something chocolate, or two. Not a paper fan.

"Sure, I've been married," he says, without being asked.

The girl doesn't know this about him.

From the last lane, the only other one in use, comes a crash and inside the crash a wonderful *thoink*. Then a bulky silence settles in.

Jack picks up another ball. He wants a thoink too. Thunder Bowl is built for noise.

"Woo woo," Susie cheers from the bench.

"Hey hey, look out for me."

"Get tough on that arm, Jack, you're still hooking. And that's free advice, leave your wallet in your pocket."

"Don't worry. I'm not."

"But listen, I used to be a pin girl."

"That," says Jack, "must've been some calendar."

Susie drinks from her cup of vodka and orange pop, her gaze wandering from Jack. A leg stretched out along the bench, an ample calf of black stocking above the green and yellow shoe. He thought she would doff the cape to bowl.

Jack takes his vodka and lemonade from the cup holder, keeping the ball in his other hand. He roams, nodding, his heels slide in the rented shoes but better that than cramped in a smaller poorly sized pair. Sliding heels cannot be good for his game.

"You're ending your visit awful quickly," he says.

"Did you just ask me to stay? Is that where this is headed? Jeepers."

At the front counter the owner tickles his arm with a straw, talks on the phone. When Jack asked him for shoes he was twiddling the straw in his ear.

"This isn't my usual day," says Jack.

"You're saying it's quite the day for you."

"Let's say that."

"I'll take that as a compliment. Though it sounds like we can hold off on the fireworks."

"How's your drink?"

"Somewhere you need to be?"

"Yeah."

Susie jiggles her cup.

"Nowhere," and Jack jiggles his cup.

"We're close then. To another drink."

"That hook, that's not me. I can bowl."

"But, Jack, I ever tell you I used to be a pin girl?"

"Which month, December?"

The bark of Jack's laugh knocks him sideways. The ball slips from his hand. He feels it slipping and realizes that down there in the loose shoe is his foot. He makes no wild grab. The ball misses, thumps floor. He laughs.

"Girl, capital P capital I capital N! Pin girl!"

This halts Jack as he is reaching for the ball.

"Where are we, the home of the deaf?" Susie throws her leg from the bench. "Thank goodness I got my hearing away from here while it was still attached to my brain."

Jack straightens. He sets the ball on the track of balls. He can walk out of here and eliminate the day. Gone, done. People tire of chasing down answers. He believes they tire too easily. He knows how he tires.

"Show me," he says.

Susie doesn't speak.

"Come on," he says.

"You want me to ask *what*, and give you all the options. But you'll be the kind who only says things he can take back."

Jack drinks. A video game whistles and squeals.

"I used to think I kept making the same mistake," he says. "But after a while it's not the same thing at all. It feels like there aren't any real mistakes left to be made. Got one you can loan me?"

He wishes she would quit looking at the ceiling. He squirms his heel down into the shoe.

"Show you what?" says Susie, finally.

"Show me how a pin girl works."

The corners of her orangey mouth curl up.

"Here's a memory. There was usually one comedian a night who wouldn't let me get quite out of the way after resetting the pins before he fired a ball."

"I can imagine."

"No," says Susie, "don't."

Then dress scarves cape she swishes by, again introducing Jack to the smell of felt. If she does say something, (and she would), he can choose what it is later.

Susie walks down the lane, a creak in one shoe. At the three standing pins she bends to look into where the lane drops off, then steps over to the next lane. With a swoop of her arm she snatches a couple pins and sets them up in their lane. She tweaks the positioning. She starts back.

"That's it?" says Jack. "That's everything?"

Susie stops. She slides her feet apart. Then, collecting folds, she draws up her long dress. Her black stockings have red knees.

"Can I trust your aim?" She is not smiling.

Jack selects a ball.

"Don't hook, Jack."

The owner is yelling. "You, what the hell."

Jack readies. He can't see any of the pins.

The sky is dusking.

"It's impossible for anyone alive to drive that slowly."

His father's voice comes from the yard. Jack looks to the door at the verandah.

"You know how worried Dar was, what was she supposed to think? Plenty, that's how much, and worry clings to her. How can she know what to expect from you? It's her daughter."

"We're safe," says Jack, walking into the yard.

Using the new shovel his father digs up a chunk of grassy ground. "It's not as if she doesn't care." He flips the chunk toward one of the many piles of chunks, wipes a hand on the short sweatshirt. "Not Dar," he says.

"This can't all be garden. You're not serious."

"Tonight seemed like my chance, I don't need a lot of light."

An idea of Jack's has her returning with her suitcase from inside the house. In the morning he drives her to Kingston, calling her by name as much as she likes. He believes she was overdoing the limp, and the rest of it, but even if they don't begin talking again they might as well go ahead and rout the night together.

"Get the pitchfork there. Start by the fence and don't be afraid to invest a little elbow juice. You're the one who crows

56

about being a gardener, you should be explaining this to me." His father pokes the shovel at the ground. "Lend your old man a hand, he's the only one you've got."

Jack walks to the pitchfork. He doesn't touch it.

"You do the pitchfork after you spread the new dirt." He can't be that wrong, it's only dirt.

"The pitchfork, c'mon, it's getting dark."

"There's an order to this."

"That's right, and if you're interested in doing half a job then what you do is dillydally like this and when nothing grows you blame the store that sold you the soil and God for being chintzy with His blasted rain. Hallelujah."

"So with this fifteen acres you're clearing you must plan on coming back here when it's time to harvest the wheat. I guess that's what you're saying, you're definitely steering in that direction."

Both of them stop.

The neighbour, and Jack doesn't try in the least for a name, has turned up at the fence. He is holding a small propane tank.

He says, "Yes, you've gone all the way up to here with your digging. Darlene, of course, will be aware of how water drains from her yard to mine, but just as long as each of us is aware of that."

Jack has a flutter in his chest. He recognizes it. His father ignores the man. On this, Jack agrees with him. They wait out the intrusion, which trails off.

Jack aims for the verandah.

His father flicks dirt at him.

"Go."

"Here I go."

"Great."

"You do the pitchfork when you're supposed to do the pitchfork and not before and not now," Jack tightens the headlock, the thick grey mess of hair, his father grunts, yanks Jack's shirt punches his leg, Jack kicks through dug-

57

up ground and his father stumbles but the headlock keeps him up, a punch then hits the button on Jack's pants and immediately Jack is convinced his father meant to drill it in lower, cold and blunt, and won't miss a second time and Jack saying, "I shouldn't be doing this, what're you doing," tucking punches under and up, through moustache.

They aren't struggling anymore.

"Okay, Jack," his father says, muffled, "okay."

But the entire waiting-room is not the same. Down near the woman wearing the housecoat and sweatpants, the cougher, the wall colour changes. More blueish.

"What time is it?" says his father.

"It's never fast at this place," says Jack.

Or it's a trick of his angle and the lighting, the change in wall colour.

"I don't have a handle on how they decide here."

"No."

"A bullet wound, a stroke, there's no question." His father continues to talk in a low voice. "But where do they draw the line and say that anything less severe than that line waits its turn? You can die from a concussion and not have a mark showing."

"You don't have a concussion," says Jack.

His father crosses, uncrosses his arms. A stale smell comes off him. The waiting-room itself smells like mouthwash.

Earlier on the muted television here rubber ducks floated by beneath the newscaster, each flying a banner with the name and age of a celebrity having a birthday. At his apartment they help one another, filling in details about the celebrities the other person is vague on, and not always because of the age. Hurry it's the ducks, the girl calls if Jack is out of the room. She plays at being concerned. He used to count on being able to do the same himself. For now, she has let herself be distracted by him.

"I didn't expect to have a son taller than me. Not even

58

when it was happening."

"That sweatshirt doesn't fit you," says Jack.

"I didn't buy it."

"Leave anything over there you have to pick up?"

"Nothing that's an emergency."

Jack pats his shirt where the button is off. The woman coughs.

"You still pray?"

"No," says Jack. "You?"

"Only when I can do it without lying."

Jack looks over. The bleeding has stopped and, from the side, the nose doesn't appear crooked.

"Me too," he tells his father.

Skin

His father arrives home carrying a large paper bag and a newspaper. He takes off his cap and places it on the shelf by the door, brim out. From the bag he pulls a leopard skin and a long dark wig. He holds the leopard skin out before him, turning it around. The skin has one arm hole, two leg holes, a zipper.

He puts the skin in the washbowl and sets the egg timer. The timer never times an egg, actually. While the skin soaks in Cheer his father opens the newspaper on the kitchen table and stands bent over it, hands cupped at his back. He looks through the box scores. His favourite players, it seems, don't play anymore.

The egg timer dings. His father scrubs the leopard skin with a brush, working in small, and even smaller, circles. Veins press up in his arms. The soap bubbles dissolve and he rinses the skin, water dripping to the floor. He steps over the water, the boy steps over it, then his father pegs the skin inside out on the clothesline and sails it into the sunshine. The boy smells warm bright summer green. In the yard sits the push mower, the wheels hidden in the grass.

His father as a T-bone steak. The rubbery suit fits snugly over his head, and as he moves it hisses and squeaks.

His father parading on the red carpet laid outside Bixdale's Meats. Streamers wave and tangle. Children take to poking the rubbery suit. They pokepokepoke when their mothers don't stop them and, at first, his father only smiles. Soon he is letting go with whinnies, poke or no poke, and winking as he offers mothers a special coupon for hamburger meat.

His father is taller than Bixdale by a head. Bixdale fills a wide, stained apron. A fire escape climbs a wall in the alley where the two men are, the bottom part of it dangling. Out at the sidewalk, at the corner of the store, brick scrapes the boy's cheek. His father keeps tugging at where the rubbery suit pinches. Bixdale doesn't return his smile. And when Bixdale pokes, it is nothing like the other pokes.

The rubbery suit leaves a ring around his father's face.

Five-fifteen Friday afternoon his father puts on his cap and the boy opens the door and they start for the Strand Theatre downtown. His father carries the suitcase with the faded Honolulu travel sticker. Packed inside the suitcase are the clean leopard skin and the wig, the leopard spots touched up with black paint, along with a towel and washcloth and bar of soap, a bathing cap to improve the fit of the wig, and a package of Spearmint Juicy Fruit Gum. The metal plates on his father's heels sound against the sidewalk. The boy always hopes for sparks.

They pass Dutchie's Drugs. Dressed in his collared white top Dutchie leans at the doorway, the usual half-smoked unlit cigar clenched in his teeth. According to the boy's father, the woman that lives with Dutchie above his store is his housekeeper. The boy's father and Dutchie nod in the general direction of one another.

The boy claims the front row in the Strand Theatre and plants himself in the middle seat. He smacks his box of McIntosh Toffee on the armrest, picks out a good piece. With where he sits he is ahead of everyone but more importantly tonight he is ahead of everyone with what he knows.

The lights dim. A flattened popcorn box wings for the curtain. The boy digs deeper into his seat. Whistling goes off behind him, then a crack of laughter that is too loud too close. They are not boys back there. They are not men yet either. They are the palaver in between. That is as close to swearing as his father ever comes, palaver. When he says the word, and he says it only at home, he says it in a quiet rush. He doesn't apologize.

A circle of light strikes the curtain. The curtain flinches

where the light hits, the boy believes he sees this, just as he believes he hears the curtain give a *mump!* Over his head hangs the dusty trail of the circle.

Drums roar. Drums chase. Wild animals shriek.

The circle of light shinnies up to a top corner of the curtain. The boy cranes his neck. All at once his father swings into view, the circle of light meeting him, catching him. He is long and serious in the leopard skin, one shoulder bare and his arms and legs wrapped around the rope, his jaw firm, and as he swings across the stage, the light nearly losing him, he leans backs from the rope and with the dark wig dancing behind him bellows a jungle call. The call squashes the drums and animals, it storms the theatre. A rolling, echoing call.

His father has disappeared. The circle of light rests on the curtain. It waits.

A scratchy popping noise becomes the drums and animals again. A jungle call is bellowed. Then his father swings back the other way, and at the middle of the curtain, straight in front of the boy, the floating boy, he releases a hand from the rope and throws out his arm and on command the curtain begins to open, the movie screen flickering inside, and coolly he continues riding the rope and the circle of light, up and off. Away.

More people enter the lobby from the theatre.

Up in the skinny fake tree, his father chews his gum. He stares out the slit in the wig, a trim of bathing cap showing. Perched above him in the tree is a stuffed monkey.

Finally his father reaches down and holds out the ads for coming attractions. He gives the leopard skin a tug. The tree groans.

A few people take an ad from the boy's father. One woman who does is familiar. The boy isn't sure why. Then he recognizes the man she is with. Smiling lightly, Dutchie watches her while she reads the ad to him. No cigar or collared top, but a powder blue ascot. Dutchie and his young housekeeper pass through the doors and into the roller-coastering light of the marquee.

The boy chews his gum. He stays ready with an extra bundle of ads. Up in the tree his father beats his chest with one slow fist then the other. His jungle call comes out short and bumpy now. The lobby is emptying. But his father keeps calling.

The Right Pieces

Guy knows someone here. Wayne can't say for sure which one. The fire spits as wood is tossed on.

Guy gives a c'mon with his head. Beneath the floppy bucket hat deep lines cut his cheeks. Wayne takes a drink from his cup.

"Winnipeg?" says a woman, laughing.

Wayne follows the dirt path away from the trailer and the lights strung between trees and the crowd of 30 or 40 that includes a male mannequin dressed in a bikini and cowboy boots. Ahead of him Guy is a dull orange shirt, as if a faint reflection of the fire. The path drops off.

Guy springs the trunk lid free of the dent. He puts on a flashlight.

"Eh? How about it?"

Tape. Rolls and rolls, electrical, masking, packing, the car trunk filled. Wayne picks up a roll, turns it in his hand. He doesn't know what to say.

"Tape," he says.

Off through the trees another camp fire flickers. Wayne can't recall the car riding with anything more than its normal slouch on the way here. In the time he has known Guy he has yet to see him without the bucket hat. Guy must want the hat to be an obvious habit.

"Not that I'm giving up dealing in stereos or like that, the high end merchandise," says Guy. "This is my busman's holiday, boy, a little of the sweet and simple. I can't name nobody who doesn't use tape. It'll fly out of here."

He pours himself more vodka-loaded orange juice, after giving the bottle a hard shake. It is half Wayne's money inside that bottle. Guy bounces on the trunk to get the lock to catch. Wayne retrieves the bottle from under the car seat and gives it a shake of his own.

Then he says, "When Frank Sinatra died they saved his

eyes. Those little cards for your wallet? He'd made his card out in secret, giving them away. So one day you don't see very well and the next you're looking with Frank Sinatra's eyes. Jesus Christ, what goes through your mind?"

A lightness has come over Wayne, and not from drinking, he refuses to sell it that cheaply. He wants to believe it has been earned.

She treats Nicorette gum like Chiclets.

"Five," says Carol, chewing. "All right?"

Sitting on the edge of the bed she plays with the clock. Glowing numbers tumble.

Wayne scratches his stomach. In the room he rents are good, long curtains, but the curtain rods in her bedroom are bare. Her air conditioner gurgles.

"You'll be fine dressing without the light and take it easy with the door, don't force or bang, I can hear every door on this whole floor. Last year an idiot used to ride his bike down the hall like it was the fucking sidewalk."

Carol shows him the alarm set for five AM.

"I'll make breakfast," says Wayne. "Got eggs?"

"Thanks but Joe gets up early to have his bowls of cereal in front of the TV. Minimum he's a year better than his friends sizewise, but I'd better not catch him ever taking advantage of it. Protecting himself is different, there's no rules then. The way Joe eats, if he was any smaller he'd be a lot bigger."

She puts on a shirt, a man's, leaves it unbuttoned. Wayne noticed it first at the factory where the temp agency sent a group of them to pack straws, how she talks to a changing spot. It can be as if she is talking to everyone, or no-one. At the factory Wayne and Guy snuck boxes of straws out to the car trunk, a trunk emptying of tape much slower than Guy predicted. Wayne may ask Carol if she needs a roll of any kind.

"He's a fisherman."

"When?" Carol says to the ceiling.

"Him," says Wayne. "Your son."

Carol doesn't answer.

"Because that's—"

"What about him?"

"—that's when they're biting. Early."

"I don't get you."

"He'd catch some, after his cereal. Fishing."

"Fishing?"

"He's up early you said. You said he likes to."

"When did I say fishing? I didn't say anything about fishing. Fishing?"

"Boys do that, they fish. I did. I do."

"Thanks but he has plenty of friends. They're always calling."

Wayne can get a shower here in the morning before she twigs to what he is up to. What he smells comes from the armpit away from her. A short while ago neither of them had any questions.

Carol drapes her leg over his.

"I'll try not to wake you," says Wayne.

"I know you will," says Carol.

Wayne feels chewing against his shoulder.

Standing by the door he finally comes up with the name. Clam diggers. Rope at the waist, calf-length legs. The pants, including the rope, are a pinkish-red white, as if bled on by other clothes in the wash.

A brick sits on a stack of newspapers. A can of WD-40 oil and a magnifying glass sit on the floor by the beanbag chair in which Nordy is slumped. Wayne won't sit.

Regularly Wayne clips grey from his temples. He has quit his chest where it is spreading quicker.

Nordy licks and seals the joint, gropes for the lighter. He spills over a pair of yellow satin shorts, most of his weight appearing to have drained into his belly. The rest of him is stringy. Limp. He speaks in a rumble.

Wayne looks through the doorway again. The cat sleeps amongst a clutter of dishes on the counter, its paw in a frying pan. He has not seen a litter box.

By coming here he has made himself part of Guy's show, an add-on. But by Wayne keeping to himself that he realizes Guy is all show means that Guy goes ignorantly on proving Wayne correct. Day after day, superiority is Wayne's.

Guy laughs but wearing those clam diggers he isn't one to be laughing. Yet it is Wayne as the punk statue, posed with the bag with the two rolls of electrical tape and box of bendable straws for Nordy. If told to leave, then he will sit.

Guy takes the joint from Nordy and folds into himself on the metal chair. A fan rushes the smoke over his bucket hat.

The newspapers stack up to Wayne's elbow. Who collects newspapers?

In the room he rents the mattress is firm, the dead bolt solid, and no-one from any of the rooms cooks cabbage or curry, no-one keeps a door open to trap company from the hall. There are the good curtains.

But a car such as the one a week ago is not left unlocked for long, or by mistake, so being finicky and first taking the money out of the appointment book it was tucked inside of would have been the mark of a fool. The flag in the parking meter was up.

Reading the appointment book of a person he will never meet is not violence. He plans to return the book, to take it from the room he rents and put it in a mailbox.

In the appointment book she crosses her sevens to avoid confusing them with her ones. He has come to picture her as tall, smooth, fair. Tomorrow, according to the book, she meets an Ellen for lunch.

Wayne has not budged from the door. He hears Guy tout the box of bendable straws as if it is the last box in the world and the beanbag chair squeals as Nordy heaves himself around toward Wayne who thinks he smells cat, damp and

67

gamey. He itches.

"Further out, Joe."

Carol motions with the bat. New, narrow sunglasses make her face pointier than Wayne believes it to be, but he likes her in the flip-flops. He peels a slice of ham from the package and dips it in the jar of mustard. They have a strip of green with a picnic table and a barbecue stand, he has decided that next time they will barbecue, and the river is near and, next time, ?shable. Traffic noise from the curve of highway overhead butts in less than he expects. All this within walking distance of Carol's. He takes off his shirt, won't worry about the grey on his chest. Soon, he will buy shorts.

Out on the strip the boy waits. His loose, sloppy clothes are streaked with names and logos. Wayne recognizes the style.

"Remember," says Carol, "squeeze the ball."

"Whack it, honey," says Wayne, and finishes the slice of ham.

There is lunge in Carol's swing, and a lateness. The ball peters out in the grass. The boy doesn't move.

"Hurry, the batter's going to first base," says Carol.

The boy's reply doesn't reach the picnic table.

"He's not fast, get him!"

"I told you, I want to practice flies." The boy swats the air with his glove.

"You're not concentrating on the what's what, Joe. Don't trick yourself like this."

When the boy does start for the ball, he wears his glove on top of his cap.

"Looks like the other team's in front," says Wayne. A swim in the river suits the day, the sun drying what clothes they choose to keep on. Rather than become a concern in the water the boy can stay here. There's food, cold drinks. He can practise being big for his age.

The boy throws the ball. It lands away from Carol.

"Hey," Wayne calls, "there used to be a one-armed player. A professional." He stops, surprised and a little uneasy with how loud he is, even with the traffic overhead. "It's true," he says to Carol. "He had this routine with his glove after making a catch. He'd get the glove off...first he'd get the ball out." The details are close. He rubs the corner of the picnic table. "It was almost as slick as if he had both arms. Of course it'd have to be."

Carol gets rid of the flip-flops and tosses the ball higher. She cuffs a grounder, then two more. Wayne encourages her by not mentioning her mistakes.

"This is a disaster," says the boy, after the next grounder.

"You think every hit in the game is going to be a juicy fly just to make Joe Kirby a happy boy? I can hit flies, I'll hit flies, I don't know where you get off thinking the way you do because it's not going to be all flies. The ball. Get it. Go, lazy guts."

"He wants everything his way," says Wayne. "Don't give it to him."

He tries reading what is spray-painted on a standard supporting the highway. It may not be lettering, it may be another logo. He understands, roughly, how a standard does what it does, which makes him the same as most people since most people keep up and keep going by knowing a few of the right pieces. Radio. He can't explain radio, yet a radio is not strange to him.

"What's that supposed to mean, everything his way?"

Carol is staring at him, sunglasses pressing into her cheeks as she chews.

"Better still, what're you even doing here with us?"

Recently Wayne has discovered her bedroom clock is ten minutes fast and gouging his five AM.

"Huh? Let's hear it."

"Where?" Wayne says, because it is no answer and exactly what he wants to give this voice of hers.

"Do you have one real reason for being here? Because I

don't have one for this anymore, whatever this is."

Things dart, prick. Wayne does not resist these things.

"Hit to the kid. Do you know what a fly is, for fuck's sake?"

"You think I won't do anything in front of him, you think you can get away with threatening me because he's here." Carol jabs the bat at Wayne. "Every chance I give you, you shit on."

Wayne dips another slice of ham, scrapes off some of the mustard.

"Huh yourself," he says, and takes a bite.

Carol, though, has turned.

"*Joe?*"

Wayne makes his way over. The boy lies flat on the ground, eyes closed and arms out wide. He is breathing.

"Nudge him," says Wayne.

"I'm not playing this stupid game, Joe."

Kneeling, Carol lugs him up into a sitting position. But the boy sinks back to the ground, though not too hard Wayne notices, the moment she releases him. Wayne wants Carol to follow through on her threat. Leave the boy here if he doesn't quit the act, then he will find out how serious she is.

The next morning on the cool, groggy walk back to his room, Wayne isn't sure which took up more of the night, sex or arguing. Maybe that isn't it at all. Maybe it's the idea that, for them, the one is not possible without the other, not any longer.

The show worsens as Guy pretends to be wrestling the newspaper clipping from his wallet, so with his knife Wayne slices open another bundle of telephone books. He loads the books from the back seat of the car into the duffel bag, not into the wheeled cart.

"Been sitting on this, incubating it." Guy wags the clipping.

Wayne ignores him.

Then he lets himself skim the clipping. A married couple won some money in a lottery. He returns the clipping and grabs telephone books.

"Appreciate what it's telling you, boy?"

"Friends of yours? Ha, I doubt it."

"Maybe they are. What do you say then? I bet you say everything a lot different is what."

"I say look at what you got out of it. A great pile of nothing."

"And I say 300 tousand," says Guy, dropping the h. "Nobody no more pays attention to a tiny 300 tousand, it has to be a full million to be a splash. Give their 300 tousand six months, like yours truly has, and it's like it never was news. I bet no noisy alarms for these people, none of that stuff. Because here—"

He snatches a telephone book from Wayne and flips through it. Then he shoves the book back at him, his finger stuck to an open page.

"Since last year's book they haven't gone nowhere."

Wayne sees a hangnail.

"Perfect strangers to me," says Guy.

Wayne lifts his duffel bag and wonders again where Guy got the wheeled cart, and if another cart was available but he wasn't told about it. So far with delivering telephone books, he can only fall behind.

Yet there he is the following night in the passenger seat of the car, in the shadow of a tree down the block from the address. The house is a bungalow, a light at the front door, if it isn't the bungalow next to it with a light but a driveway on the opposite side.

"April," says Guy, hand shielding his mouth, "new roof."

Wayne draws his arm in from the window. He can feel where the telephone books have pulled on his shoulders.

"May," says Guy, "a Toyota. Now she has a hers like he has a his."

Wayne hears crickets. Crickets are his sound of quiet. But

it is just bugs in the grass and if something about the sound of quiet seems important then he is likely exaggerating, or misunderstanding himself, and also he cannot believe he is the only one who has tried to make crickets be the sound of quiet. There can't be anything personal about it, not if it is a copy, even one by accident.

"I took Drummond to get here," says Guy.

Wayne watches the house.

"Nothing happened on Drummond. But what, hey, if I took Belmont instead?"

"We can't stay here," says Wayne, "it looks bad."

"A no-brain runs the red on Belmont and crashes me. But on Drummond, nothing, while over on Belmont no-brain ran an empty red. Eh? You want to know about that kind of luck. You want to count it up and you can't, but there's lots of it out there, boy, has to be. The luck you don't know you have is probably your best luck of all."

The crickets carry on.

"I don't know Belmont," says Wayne.

"Why them?" Guy says into his hand.

"I don't like what if," says Wayne. "It's usually late."

On the drive back Guy takes Belmont. If he pulls his bucket hat any lower the road will be nothing but a hiss of tires to him, so Wayne counts off the numbers on the houses. It isn't necessary to be able to read all the numbers.

The curtains, snuck out in his duffel bag, become a credit at a secondhand store. It is not as if he spends much time in the room. At night there he undresses by the thin light from outside and hides his wallet inside his shoe. The sun is not rising as early in the morning.

The intercom in her building sizzles at him.

"Who?"

Her voice, however, has never been very clear on the intercom.

"Wayne." Then he says, "Me."

"I don't know any Wayne." This after a pause.

"I'm glad you're home," he says, just the same. "Surprise."

The woman tells him twice, first through the intercom and then through the space between frame and apartment door, from behind the chain, her lipstick black.

Next he hears it from the recording over the pay phone. Then a live operator can't, or won't, locate Carol for him.

"What do you mean?" he says, until the operator disconnects him.

Foot twisting and hip jutting Nordy flubs the step down yet lands upright on the sidewalk outside The Royal.

Across the street, Wayne stops.

Nordy steadies himself. He undoes his pants and pushes in his shirt, fastening the pants again below his belly, a flap of shirt missed. Then, with almost delicate strokes, he checks if he needs a shave.

Wayne wears shorts. His legs are too stumpy for shorts, his knees crowd his feet. He knew this before but during the actual buying of the shorts he knew it less. He failed to get in his own way. Shorts, he wanted them.

Further along he crosses the road and keeps tailing. The humid air coats his skin. They are not alone on the street. Nordy weaves, coughs.

Where's the cat sleeping? says Wayne.

Now on the stairs up to his apartment, Nordy plants himself back against the wall. He squints down at Wayne on the bottom step.

Wayne has figured it out. The wallet card let Frank Sinatra believe he was getting away with a cheat, because how easily he could die facing the wrong direction, distracted by an uproar, a promise, by something that had nothing to do with him. The wallet card doubled his chances for a proper last look. Frank Sinatra lived better because of the card.

Then the day Guy says, One suitcase for each of them in her Toyota, boy, Wayne meets back up with him at night and at the bungalow a basement window gives. The floor inside is further down than either of them expects. Guy picks up his flashlight, clicks it on and off. Wayne tests his ankle, chews his gum.

In the bedroom the curtains are shut and Wayne takes a sports jacket from the closet. It fits large but large is wearable. He searches with his penlight. Ties hang in a row on the closet door. On the floor both pairs of shoes have shoe trees.

At their age, they can't be an every night in here, says Guy. So who of them is it, who begs who with a pretty please? Who dogs who?

And he sniffs and howls.

Wayne roots through dresser drawers. Clothes scatter. He finds a harmonica and slides it into the pocket of the sports jacket where his knife is. He will learn, he will practise, maybe he is meant to play an instrument.

Then, to Wayne, the scent from the perfume bottle Guy sprays is violet. He imagines a mauve cloud. He dangles a sock drawer by the handle. It seems ridiculous, a drawer named for socks.

Guy lies on the bed, the flashlight aimed straight up from his stomach. He makes a shadow animal on the ceiling. He goes on boasting. He is almost singing.

Wayne's arm tremors. The boasting chases at him.

He hopes the sports jacket is tweed. Tweed is nice.

But you see? I'm a winner here too, boy, not just them. I'll choose what they would like to donate as my share.

Bright and raw the words leap from Wayne. I wouldn't care even if this was your mother's.

Nobody does this to his mother, nobody who's not garbage. That's not me.

The shadow animal yaps its mouth. Or are those wings?

Not me, says Wayne.

Only the flashlight jumps from the bed. Guy is slow for his age. The sock drawer has broken on his face.

First, Wayne's knife hits rib. Without light the bedroom still glistens.

When it is over it is as if he is already there, hovering, waiting, cleanly ahead of himself for the most part. He can't smell violet.

He showers in the dark with a new bar of soap and decides that Guy's sister is large like her husband. One of the reasons they stay married, and stay in this bungalow, is because they share a largeness. *That*, he decides, is their luck. It is a luck they know about.

If they meet Wayne, they will not blame him for what he could not know.

He swallows the gum and gargles with Listerine. He matches clean clothes to the sports jacket, a belt fixing the pants at his waist as he dresses in the hall. His old clothes and the bucket hat fit in a grocery bag.

He parks the car. In the rented room his suitcase and duffel bag are packed. That much he planned. His timing, then, at last, is improving. He places a five dollar bill under the room key, for the curtains.

Letting Nordy bumble up into his apartment, untouched, unmarked, eyes still seeing, now that must be worth something too.

JOEL KATELNIKOFF

Notes on the Apocalypse

The police station: a moonlit tower of iron and brick. I remove my mittens, press my palms against it. Brick and glass litter metal streets. When the night air numbs my fingers, I turn from the building and head for shelter.

The metal streets: no cars, no people. I creep down barren sidewalks like frost over glass.

Fire! Flames eat my living-room! A moment ago, calm. Now, fire! The living-room turns to kindling. I want to put it out, but I find the flames too repulsive.

An Ending: I will buckle on my skis and slowly head out, rusty shards of metal sparkling under the moon's light.

SCIENCE AXIOM: *Factors A B and C feed into situation X, yielding result Z (apocalypse).*

There will be scavengers!

I have a small wooden house. The exterior is old and unre-markable, but the inside is exquisite. The walls are covered in paintings by local avant-garde artists, some of which seem very forward-thinking. In this city, it was once considered in poor taste to use colour in a nightscape, since human eyes cannot actually see colour in near-dark. Rods and cones, etc. I have sought quality art and I have found it.

The radio stations: no reception at all now. At every frequency in the spectrum, AM and FM, nothing. No signal. No emergency broadcast message. No way to know what's going on.

My nightlamp flickers out. Now the moon lights my room. Every star in the cloudless sky reflects off my mirror and off the metal streets.

A dream: I lie face down, arms outstretched. My body sinks into the grass.

My labours at present: Seek out the food (the edible stuff) and gather it all at a central location. Or spread it out over several places in case the scavengers try to get it. Then, find anything useful that is not fire-destroyed. Guard it. If necessity demands, venture out. Only if necessity demands.

Inventory: Shelves of canned food. Beans, tomatoes, corn, soups. Soups of every variety. There is a lot of canned food, enough to ready me for anything. And lots of unmarked cans, all silver with no labels. Eat the marked cans first. Number the unmarked ones with a black marker. Now at least I won't eat the same can twice.

One other human being exists. He lives next door. He scares me. He looks at maps. Maps of this city and all of its metal streets. He is map crazy!

Fire! Within this display case sits my collection of bijou art objects. The case is on fire now, burning so quickly! I reach in and pull one out: a small sapphire-encrusted butterfly. Hot! It burns me. While I writhe, explosions sound in other rooms. The living-room caves in, so I head for the kitchen.

A human being lives in a neighbouring house. I had never noticed him. Now, I find it difficult to ignore him. I look at his face, his smirk and squinting eyes. I recognize this expression, one that I myself use when pretending to admire someone I truly despise. He uses this even though we are the last two people in the world. I don't suppose we'll be friends.

A new history: Some things are important. The vast majority is not. My history starts at the beginning of time: result Z (apocalypse). Have you heard of the *ABC* theory? As for the rest, there's nothing worthy of the history books today. Same as usual, for what one must now consider usual.

The bedroom closet, I open the door. Clothes, all clothes. I want to try them on, mostly covered in soot and ash. Mostly burned or melted. Socks, pants, button-up shirts, pyjamas, ties, black shoes, slippers, blouses...blouses?

The city in the day resembles an oven element with its naked heat. Broken chromium streets sear with cracking embers of gypsum and asphalt. Noon. Everywhere, remnants of buildings that used to fill the city.

With ash and rain, the mudwasps invade. They bite and sting, unprovoked. I share my house with them now.

The anguish machine gives me light, defies the natural order of night and day. It is easy to defy natural order.

Fire! The flames burn through everything. The roof and wall of the living-room collapse. So I pray. I pray for rain. I say AMEN and the clouds explode. Boom. End of fire. Water and mud fill the room. I can see the bushes in the front yard. The ravaged room expands throughout the entire world.

The bijou art object, it exactly resembles a butterfly. Made of silver and decorated with sapphires, it is a butterfly in every respect except that it does not live. My hand bears the bijou's imprint in blistered skin.

Other than trying to survive, I am startlingly unoccupied. I dedicate a whole night to breaking things. I shatter all of the windows at the police station, but when I realize that they will never be replaced, the action seems empty.

My skis grind against the cold metal streets, white crescent moon cutting through the black veneer of night.

Inventory: The living-room and bedroom are destroyed entirely. In the other rooms, everything is heat-damaged. The aerosol cans in the bathroom have all blown up. There is foam and hairspray and sticky stuff everywhere. The kitchen and basement. Chairs, table, cans, a bottle of wine! Porno magazines in the basement. The scavengers must be aware of this, and I am afraid.

My labours at present: To peel back a few floorboards. This opens a fifteen-foot drop into the basement. The scavenger will die on impact, or at least shatter bone.

The mudwasps have a surprisingly polite demeanor. I have learned a lot about them through their body language and the frequency of buzzing wings. I take all of their actions at face value. When they are not biting me it is because they are already full. So I share my food with them.

There was once a front door, where visitors would knock before daring to enter. These days, no-one will knock. Now, visitors go through open walls like ghosts. If I am the only person left in the world,

Writing a new history: Human beings have made such importance of their life and times. But really, is anything worth it? As I see it, these times are more usual than usual. There is nothing special about these times. That could be the beginning and the end of my book.

Snow: The stuff that once came from the sky and would land

on the street. Streets of pavement, streets of gravel. Summer days of long prairie highways lined with wheat and canola, carbon, water, clouds, cows, towns and cities! Winter snow, fur-lined parka hoods, toques, horses and sleighs, and cross-country skis for travelling to cottages with fireplaces.

My neighbour keeps appearing! His house is destroyed and miserable and full of vermin. "More than enough supplies," he tells me. He asks if I would like to share or trade. I know better than to fall for this trick. There will be no trickery, no tricks, no games. My neighbour is my enemy and I make no secret of this.

A dime. It has fallen from my pocket and into a crack in the floor. I head down to the basement and look for it. I need to find those candles.

A person? A woman? I have found things in the bathroom. Therefore, a woman. I find myself missing her, without being able to remember a single thing about her.

This city, I search through it. I remember fondly the green trees. I walk on metal streets and I can see through them. There are no metal streets. There is nothing beneath them. The metal is hollow, and I have touched the sky.

The basement is full of five-gallon pails of potatoes. There is a cistern. The whole thing is grey and dark. I can't find my dime. The potatoes taste good.

Nightmare! There was no fire. Fire is a scientific lie, an elaborate hoax. It has never existed and never will. Fire is a secret. The absence of fire is a secret. Every thing that does not exist is a secret.

My neighbour wants my butterfly. He asks me to listen as he

strikes his wife repeatedly. I close my eyes, hear raised voices, sounds of a struggle, striking, screaming, wailing. But through all of this, I hear no voice but his. He has no wife.

My stomach. Potatoes in my intestines. I don't feel good about this world. I don't feel that it's real.

The mudwasps control the bathroom. When I excrete, they bite my exposed flesh. Luckily, I have lots of empty jars. I fill them and deposit them in the bathroom as gifts.

Reasons Why I Stay Here: I refuse to leave these tokens behind. I refuse to let these events change me. I must re-establish my regular routine. Home is where the heart is. Quitters never prosper.

Inventory: Weapons! A hatchet. A crowbar. An autographed hockey stick. A strange set of kitchen knives: half a dozen paring knives and one huge cleaver. If a new race evolves, will they peel back the streets? Will they skate on ice? Will they value an autographed stick?

The metal streets, the blue sparks flying in the night, they might as well be the lights of heaven.

Knitting is my most nearly mastered of the human arts. My old blankets and bedsheets are now stitched together to form giant, all-consuming units of fabric. I drape these over the rubble, hang them from makeshift frames. These are the new walls of my house, designed to protect me from the hotness of day, the coldness of night, and the treachery of scavengers.

I touch the grass, run my fingers through the grass. I caress the stones. I kiss the marble.

The neighbour peers in through my knitted walls, red eyes

glowing through the dark. At this, I leap from the melted couch, slashing at him with the hockey stick. The blade rips skin from his face.

The least natural things? Language, philosophy, science, psychology, sociology. Human beings, unless conditioned to become unnatural, will be wild, uncommunicative, and in every sense alone. The artifice of social interaction is predicated on self-deceit and the subsequent deceit of others.

I wring his neck with my bare hands. I look at his languishing eyes, dark orbs choking in their sockets.

Inventory: barely anything is missing. No orange juice in the house, but there is apple juice. No pepper. Nowhere to sleep (both the couch and the bed are ruined). No other human beings in the world.

Letters flood in from my friends. They want to know how I'm doing. I'd like to reply, "Not bad, and you?" but I'm not ready to talk to them. They are all dead now, and I'm still not sure how to break the news.

Nightmare! There was no fire, only orange and red pillars, secrets, pictures I was never meant to see, ears, pills, and honey.

Writing a new history: Earth, being so barren, has become a moon, white and rocky.

His flesh I've cut into strips and smoked over a small flame.

The sound never ends. A different kind of buzzing emanates from each corner of the world. The generator hums. The mudwasps buzz. Even in silent corners, I hear voices whispering in my ears.

My labours extend through the metal streets. I search through houses for anything resembling food. Vermin scurry too fast. All of the houses seem to have been scavenged. All by my neighbour, before I consumed his body?

I sift through piles for scavengable materials. I take nothing. I look at the rocks and bricks and sticks, the destroyed buildings, and they seem barely real to me. I cannot appreciate them, not with my finest senses. Not with sight and touch. I want to become the air around them, become the world, become every atom. And yet, I am the culmination of the atoms within my own body and scarcely understand myself.

My neighbour looms over my sleeping body. I sense his presence and leap to my feet. He attacks. Knuckles slam into my skin. He beats me with a club and kicks me in all of my organs. He beats me to death. He breaks me down into my constituent parts. He keeps beating me, beyond death, beats my spirit, beats it back into my body, beats me back to life, beats me until I'm in my prime, beats me healthier than I've ever been.

Who was this? I enter the flaming door, and she is waiting there for me, her body splashed across the floor. I collect her with buckets and mops. Her bones in a pile, I keep the skull hidden beneath ribs.

The mudwasps. The closer I get the more they sting. They have taken over the whole house and given the bathroom back to me. It is nice in here, probably nicer than all the other rooms put together, except for the wasp excrement that covers every surface.

On the left ski I draw a mountain range, each peak, each tree, each flake of snow. On the right ski, I draw a map of the city's metal streets and alleys. I flip them over and colour the bottoms. I draw the oceans and seas of the world and every single fish. I draw the crescent moon, all the stars, and all the stars' satellites.

Nightmare! There was no fire. I pull back the knitted wall and see a real wall behind it. I pull back the real wall and see my neighbour at work in his front yard. He waves hello and invites me over for beer. We make awkward attempts at conversation, exchange glances, and spend long periods of time staring at nothing in particular. I feel too uncomfortable to leave.

The bijou butterfly tries to fly away. I clench it in my hands. The wings beat, scraping my skin with sapphires.

Who has not seen time elapse, trees growing and changing like puffs of vapour, now brown, now green? Who has not seen buildings rise up faint and fair and then pass like dreams? White snow has flashed across the world and vanished, followed by the bright brief green of spring. And then the grey clouds were swept aside and vanished like the trailing garments of a ghost. There has been no cloud since, no matter how quickly the time has passed.

I have experimented with time and invented an eight-hour day. Now my life doesn't pass so slowly. I sleep for three hours and wake for five. The day is hot and the night is cold.

Who was this? Someone who found me in the garage, heart just beating. Someone who walked back out the door, closing it as she left. From that point, I lived only to spite her.

I don't feel the need to define things anymore. That's for language and human interaction. Humans, language, philosophy. It's all social.

Nightmare! There was no fire. It is bright and happy day. I'm feeling so good that I'm feeling like nothing. Ice cream in my hand. It falls off the cone and lands in the grass. Now I've ruined the grass and my ice cream both. I want to kill myself, but I can't move my arms. I run, I run through heavy traffic, but I can't get hit by anything. Not even close.

The ghosts groan. When I sleep they are here, lurking in the sinks and bushes.

My house is different than when I left. The knitted walls torn, most of my food gone. They left the unmarked cans behind.

Who was this? On a mattress in a warehouse, a yellow stained thing, naked, body blue and mouldy, yellow stained body, mattress naked, in a warehouse, blue and mouldy, on fire.

Knives are sapphires. Wasps and fur-lined remains. In the desk I used, draw, draw fingers! The face, touch it. Touch it. Oh!

Stations: special streets, my hatchet in cold drawers. I protect butterfly metal as anything I cut myself with. Metal neighbour, die on, win. Barren world, generous streets, parka hood up.

Nightmare! And now she is gone.

I've thrown away the history book. In the future, there will be no past.

I ski down metal streets, tumble toward the ground. Metal shards everywhere.

Through my window: myself walking away, down gravel, branches sprinkling rusty leaves far on the horizon.

Snow: little white things that fall on the street and on my face.

Fireworks at the Fair

1.

There is a red and white tent, a huge red and white tent. Within, there are straw bales, banners, ladies in dresses. There are chairs & tables, long tables with tablecloths, red and white. Everything is red and white. The ladies' dresses are red and white. The sweetheart cookies are red and white. The straw bales are yellow. The grass is green.

It is a beautiful summer afternoon, every contestant in her Sunday dress.

A man in a top hat walks from table to table, sampling each entry. His tongue cracks flaky crusts and tastes apple compote, ripe rhubarb & crabapples, chokecherry jam. Plum jelly leaves a trail all the way down his throat.

Top-hat salivates, munches, swallows. As he tastes each slice, each loaf, he feels the blue ribbon in his breast pocket, throbbing against his heart. The ribbon is reserved for Aunt Marnie's Famous Pudding. Aunt Marnie has won the contest eight years in a row, and she is favoured to win it again. At the far end of the tent, she lingers, watching Top-hat make his way.

Entry 24: zucchini jam, made by Helen Atamanenko. Jam watery. Zucchini crunchy.

Entry 25: Saskatoon berry pie, made by Pauline Colleaux. Crust overbaked. Filling consistent. Berries under-ripe.

Entry 26: sour pickles, made by Edith Vereshagin. Firm. Crisp. Juicy. Sour. *Too sour?* No, just sour enough.

Entry 27: a mysterious vial of red fluid. Entrant unknown.

Top-hat pauses. He strokes his impeccably waxed moustache and the blue ribbon in his pocket. He clasps entry 27, the vial's rim dusted with a bitter yellow powder. It makes Top-hat squirm, numbs his tongue before he's even tasted the liquid.

He looks to the women, who gaze at him as if he's a conjurer about to perform a trick. Top-hat does not want to drink the vial, but he can feel their collective will pressing him forward, irresistibly. He knows that a contest judge must behave like a contest judge; he has to appear resolute, know his own mind, do definite things. Top-hat smiles, gestures with his arm, and drinks deeply.

His body falling, he gropes at his pockets wildly. His chest constricts, his throat too. Where is it, he wonders. Where is it?

His hand is the last thing to hit the ground. It falls from breast pocket, clutching the ribbon. As the contestants argue over the significance of Top-hat's final action, Aunt Marnie storms from the tent, into the carnival crowd.

2.

Chuck reads the midway, head down, looking for a ground score. He discovers coins, cigarettes (only half-smoked), and dozens of bottles and cans. The ride jockeys look at him from the Carousel, the Tilt-a-Whirl, Spinning Teacups.

Chuck discovers an unused ride ticket. Chuck discovers a quarter in the dust. Chuck discovers a girl's shoe. He discovers her shapely ankle, knee, thigh, white dress. He lifts the white dress with his fingertips. Chuck discovers a punch in the face, delivered by the girl's boyfriend. He flees. The boyfriend gets back to work, trying to knock down three milk bottles with an underweight softball.

The girl is sixteen. She wants her boyfriend to win her the big stuffed bear so she has something to remember him by when he dumps her for her best friend. The boyfriend is on the school football team, so he's good at throwing stuff.

He tosses the ball. Milk bottles come crashing down. Her face lights up.

As the girl points at pink plush, the booth operator gestures at the small print on the prize chart. The boyfriend has won nothing yet—just a ticket to the semi-finals.

The operator jumps the counter and runs out to the freak show tent. He returns, accompanied by King Hercules and General Tom Thumb.

The boyfriend throws first, knocking the bottles down. The girl is ecstatic. King Hercules throws next, knocks them down. The girl is disappointed. General Tom Thumb knocks them down. The girl is bored.

"Well, gentlemen, it looks like we have a three-way tie!"

The boyfriend asks: "What now?"

"A footrace, my friend! Around the perimeter of the fair! Down through the games, the rides, exhibition tent, ticket booth, snack stands, grandstand, the lot behind the trailers, and right back here. Got that?"

The boyfriend kind of nods. The other two have run this race before.

And they take off, sprinting neck-and-neck through the skill games, gambling booths, kiddie rides. The boyfriend, being an all-star wide receiver, is confident in his ability. The three rush past the exhibition tent (red and white). General Tom Thumb is startlingly quick, takes the lead. They round the ticket booth, brushing past a line of kids with handfuls of quarters. King Hercules is a few strides back now and falling further behind. They weave through food vendors, customers, hamburgers, hot dogs. The boyfriend is getting tired now, panting and puffing. They pass the grandstand, roadies performing soundchecks to empty bleachers. General Thumb is slowing down, the boyfriend is catching up. They reach the muddy back lot behind the trailers. The boyfriend closes in on Thumb. The little General turns, lunging at him, knocking him off his feet. King Hercules catches up and pummels the boy with his fists, misting the air with blood. Thumb lets out a maniacal little laugh, cheering at knuckles bouncing off ribs.

By the time the boyfriend trails blood to the softball stand, the girl is nowhere to be found. By the look on the operator's face he can tell that she's already back at home, a pink plush bear in her arms and fresh semen in her vagina.

3.

As the sky fades to night, Virginia's eyes become the bluest thing there. There, of course, being the Ring Toss booth. She pockets a five-dollar bill, gives fifteen blue rings to a mother and her twelve-year-old son. Rings fly. Mother and son walk.

Virginia eyeballs passers-by, picks a mark, readies her voice.

"Don't blow your pipes, kid. Take a break." Chester leans on his cane. "You're doing good tonight."

"Thanks, Chester." She leans up against the counter and starts to flip through her bankroll.

"Kid, 'tis time you learned the nuances of this fair. You've got simple charm, but you don't yet know the subtleties of running this booth."

"Don't worry Chester. I know what I'm doing."

"It never hurts to hear it once more. First you learn your pitch. Different cracks work on different marks. You got your cake eaters and your sharpies. Make sure you know the difference. Then you got your prizes: the plush, which you don't give away, and the slum, which you do. And sometimes when it's real slow, you throw stock to get a draw, and then when you got a big crowd, you just go wild and burn the lot. And never interrupt a boy arguing with his girl. He'll break your nose. But if his girl's arguing with him, he'll play just to get her off his back. Are you getting all this, kid? This is the fruit of knowledge I'm passing down to you here."

"Chester, look at all these people. We should be selling rings to 'em."

He moves in closer. "Let me tell you something, kid. For you, one day I'm going to make something real. One day I'll get us out of this booth, buy us a giant wheel, six seats in each car, sixty cars on the wheel, two hundred feet in the sky. You know what we could see from two hundred feet up?"

She'd never thought about it.

"We could see a lot, kid. You and me. Two hundred feet is a long way. We could see so clear that we'd know everything. We could do anything. I promise you, kid. What I'm saying is true. It's gonna happen."

His tattoos accentuate the wrinkles of his skin. He coughs and chews a handful of amphetamines. The sky is almost black now.

"Chester, we just lost a dozen marks."

He struggles for words. "You mean, while I was talking to you? But I only counted twenty people walk by. That's four, maybe six marks."

"It was more like thirty, and I could have turned ten of 'em, Chester."

"Oh, yeah. And another thing. Never eat cotton candy in the rain."

4.

The fat lady sits down to supper.

Soup: green turtle soup (*diet* green turtle soup).

Salad: tomatoes, carrots, peas, peppers, beans, kale, squash, melons, pumpkins, and freshly harvested Jerusalem artichoke.

Main course: A tartar steak, cooked purslane leaf, brussels sprouts, broccoli, swiss chard, sauerkraut, fresh caviar, fried chicken, fig paste, meatloaf, roast duck, raw salt pork, a side of backfat, venison, elk, mountain sheep, antelope, twelve suet dumplings, seven lobsters, a pair of canvasback ducks, a double-serving of terrapin, a quantum loaf, eighteen yards of black pudding, 400 pigeons. A pie filled only with birds that can imitate the human voice. A Babe Ruth rookie card. The magazine rack from the doctor's office. A tin of motor oil. Lightbulbs. Razor blades. A human baby. Leo Tolstoy's gravestone. A space ship. Two diamond mines. Six of the seven ancient wonders of the world, excluding the Colossus. The Roman alphabet. The invisible man. Heaven. Magic. Her own skull. The rings of Saturn.

To drink: a proper wine.

After supper: pies in her pie-hole, corn dogs in her corn-hole, lady fingers in her lady-hole.

5.

It is night. The lights of the Duck Pond illuminate a garbage barrel, its lid shaped like a clown's head.

Baby Boy staggers from the Gravitron, clutches the clown's cheeks and puts his face in the barrel's great open smile.

Saliva spills from Baby Boy's mouth like sun-spoiled gelatin. Then there is a churning, chugging, expanding, contracting. His throat tenses, epiglottis seals shut. His abdomen turns pressure tank, his esophagus a metal plumbing pipe.

Flush. A strawberry Sno-Cone and half a mustard corn dog spray out through his mouth and nose. The face eats what Baby feeds it. It receives. Baby Boy gives. Seconds pass. Throat stretching. Lungs starving. Face red. Eyes bulging. Seconds turn into minutes, and finally—he is released.

Baby Boy slides down the clown, onto his knees. As stomach acids dance in his sinuses, his head grows dizzy. For a moment he is euphoric, in the womb, never been born. How can Baby Boy be sure he's alive, or ever has been?

Kites and comic-books become irrelevant. Baby smiles. Curled up on the ground, he's one foot in paradise. He will never be this high again, though he will try with drug and with woman. Even seconds from now, when his vomit gushes anew, such ecstasy will elude him.

Stupefied, Baby hears his dad lecturing the lonely Duck Pond carny. He says, "That foam reminds me of the last time I drank Guinness. I spent the night with an Irish whore, woke up in a state of sleep paralysis. I puked in my own face until I almost drowned. Lucky the whore woke up, or I'd be dad for sure."

"Did you say *dad*?" asks the carny.

"Oh, did I? Ha. I meant *dead*."

Baby Boy remembers early mornings when his mother would wake him up, wrap him in his blanket, and take him in the car while she drove dad to the factory. On the way home, she would let him sit in the front seat.

6.

Everyone has a giant foam hand and a giant beer. A rock and roll band plays rock and roll in the outdoor grandstand.

Over the loudspeakers the singer yells: "Tonight the earth will quake and the sky will rain fire! All right babies, one two three four!"

As the band launches into their rock epic, *The Strange Adventures of Maxwell Seed*, stage-mounted cannons fire streamers into a 30-foot dirt gulf between the stage and the bleachers. Sonic distortion bombards the crowd. They go wild and claw at the wire fence.

It starts to rain, a monsoon. The dirt gulf goes muddy. The band runs around the stage, throwing plastic sheeting over the mixing board, monitors, amps. As they do this, they continue to play exquisitely. The guitar player slips on the wet stage, but rising to his feet he hammers out the finest solo ever heard.

The crowd climbs over one another to get closer to the music. The sun emerges and floods the grandstand with rainbows.

The bass player feeds on the crowd's energy and is driven to spectacle. He smashes his guitar against the stage six times and flings it through the air. It lands in a pool of knee-deep mud.

They break through the fence and spill out into the slick rainbow-mud, swarming the broken guitar. Those who slip are promptly trampled. The scene reminds the drummer of his tour of duty and sends him into a flashback state.

He leaps up to fight for his life. He casts his drumsticks at the crowd, but this only pleases and encourages them. He pulls a set of throwing knives from his belt and kills five with perfect accuracy. He shoots fireballs from his fingertips, lasers from his eyes, and bullets from his gun.

The crowd tries to retreat, but he's killing them too fast. The other band members try to calm him down. "Don't touch me!" he yells, growing gasoline wings that fly him off into the stratosphere.

The survivors offer first aid to the wounded and Christian burials to the dead. The band and their roadies start to pack up, because they can't finish the show without a drummer.

Then the drummer flies back, a strafing run, firing machine guns and spraying napalm, agent orange, and mustard gas all over the place. Everyone's burning alive.

Lick hammers buttons and cranks the joystick.

"Do you think he'll beat the game?"

"I don't know, I've never seen anybody make it this far on one quarter."

"I don't think he'll make it."

"I don't know."

Lick has the heart of a lion and the will of a jaguar. He, ten years old, is a video game scientist. His hand-eye coordination is so well-developed that someday he'll be a surgeon, or a carny, or maybe both.

The Yakuza are betting $100M that Lick will win. The Sicilian Mafia are betting against him. Everything else in the arcade tent has come to a halt. Lick swivels the joystick counter-clockwise and the drummer flies in for another run. He presses a six-button combination and the flaming crowd shoots an anti-aircraft missile into the sky. The drummer is hit. The crowd is on fire. Their souls are leaving their bodies. Ghosts drift around the fairground.

Something occurs to Lick: the code of universal existence. It comes to him instinctively, in the form of a mathematical equation. He renders this equation into a 50-button video game manoeuvre. The dying crowd begins to dissipate, the drummer likewise. The world grows calm. Every object in the game is broken down to its atomic elements, most of which look very similar to cats and/or butterflies. Source code splashes across the screen and cascades to the ground. Lick has won. As always, he has won. The spectators want to embrace him, but he's already disappeared.

The Mafia pay the Yakuza with an oversized $100M cheque, seizing the photo op. Cameras: *Click-clack*!

7.

It is time for fireworks. The fuse-lighter lights fuses. People gather for the spectacle.

A carny clutches his chest. "I'll be all right, kid. Keep tossin'

99

rings."

Yellow, purple, and green comets shoot into the sky, exploding with beautiful large chrysanthemum bursts.

The carny walks behind the trailers, searching for fresh air. In the back lot he staggers, slips to the ground, and splashes through the sky.

There is a white crackle, red crackle, blue crackle, and multi-burst flower patterns with passionate barrage, covering a range of view wide as wheatfields.

Were these lights always up here? He can smell each chemical, each colour illuminating the ground below.

Magnesium, a dress, pale skin, the handle of a knife hidden behind a concession stand.

Lithium carbonate, a shattered vial, candy apples, the awning of a tent.

Copper chloride, a five-dollar bill, his tattoo, her blue eyes.

She picks her mark, delivers her pitch, takes in money, doles out slum. It will be hours still before she drops the awning.

The ambulance arrives, flashing red and white, paramedics loading up the body.

He can taste the black powder.

He can feel himself turn to smoke.

There is a typewriter in front of me. So I type:

```
Roy started work at the Planetary Department
of Finance (PDF) on Janus 22, 2305 CE. They
stuffed him in an empty office with a stack of
books in the centre. Nobody told him what his
job was, how he was going to get paid, where
to park his space-car, how to find the space-
washrooms, or anything like that. All he knew
was that a stack of space-books sat before
him. He began thumbing through the space-
pages. (NOTE-Space-noun motif doesn't seem to
be working. Edit this paragraph later.)
```

There is a typewriter in front of me. I am in an office on the top floor. I don't have anything important to do this afternoon. There is a stack of paper on my desk and a fresh black ribbon in the typewriter. So I type:

```
After three hours, Roy needed to use the wash-
room. He walked past other offices and tried
to ask employees for directions, but nobody
would turn their eyes from their desk or
acknowledge his presence in any other way.
```

There is a typewriter in front of me. Who am I? A person in an office. My office is on the top floor, or should be, if the building were inverted. I am actually twenty storeys under-ground. I sit motionless at my desk. I don't have anything important to do this afternoon and I can't remember an afternoon when I did. There is a stack of paper on my desk. There is a ribbon in the typewriter. My heart is a pool of eels. Only the clacking of keys will fill this silence. So I type:

Eventually, he found a dark oily room. He relieved himself down a hole in the floor and snuck back to the room with nothing but books. Most were technical manuals, no two on the same subject. There were manuals on insulin research, ferris wheel construction, bijou art object repair, etc.

Later, he went home for the evening.

I think this story is really going somewhere. I show it to my best friend, the quiet guy in the corner. He scans the story line by line, page by page. He spits it back at me. Now he has replicated my story. He is either flattering or mocking me, I can't tell which. My best friend is a photocopier. My other friends are also machines. As far as I can recall, I've never encountered anything else.

In his living quarters, Roy consumed energy and rested his body.

The next day he found that all of the books in his office had been replaced with new ones.

Smiling in fear, he wondered if they had been replaced right after he went home, or just before he came back.

I'd like to show this story to my boss. I gather the typewritten pages and rise from my desk. I realize I've never seen him and don't know how to find him, so I sit back down. Maybe I could fax him? I do have a fax machine, but I only use it as a friend. "Would you like something to eat?" I ask it as I pull a celery from beneath my desk. No response. The celery is warm and limp. It's difficult to eat it this way. I think it gives me energy. Maybe it doesn't.

Roy's spirit began to atrophy. He could rarely

stir up enough courage to leave the room, and
on those rare occasions he would move in
stealth.

I open and close my mouth, making some sounds. There is a
telephone at my desk. I believe that pressing 0-0-0-0-0-0-0-
0-0-0 may do something. I put the receiver against my face
and hear a noise.
"Operator, how may I direct your call?"
"Wow, what does that mean?"
"Sir, can I help you?"
"Maybe. I mean, I hope you can."
"What can I do for you, sir?"
"Well, I'd like to talk to someone."
"Who would you like to talk to?"
"Someone. A real person. I want to have a real friend."
"Wouldn't we all, sir, wouldn't we all."
"Are you a real person?"
"I'm sorry, sir. I'm under strict company orders not to
disclose that information."
"What company do you work for?"
"I'm under strict orders not to disclose that information
either."

As Roy was reading about advanced ergonomics,
the building's power shut off. The room went
dark. The ergonomics book dissolved in his
hand. Roy ran out into the empty hallway.
There was nobody in the neighbouring office,
or the next. Roy went through the entire
floor. As he arrived at the reception area,
the lights came back on. A secretary material-
ized behind the desk.

I dream my office has a window. A blackbird flies across and
lands on the ledge. She looks into my eyes and sings. I stop

typing. My ears are flooded with melodious trills and crotchets. With each phrase of her song she draws me nearer. I am on my knees, up against the glass, wanting to touch her. Crescendos and glissandos are pouring out of her mouth. I fall. I quiver. I chirp. Soon I too am a bird. Our melodies intertwine.

I look up and see that she is gone. Silence. There is no window.

```
"This is not a real person. It is a hologram."
Roy's hand passed through the secretary.
```

I'm tired. Either I've just woken up or I'm about to fall asleep. I ask the fax machine and the photocopier, "Is it a good idea for Roy to realize that he's in a world of holograms and that he is in fact a robot?" The photocopier responds glibly. The fax machine interjects. Then the photocopier again, then the fax. They are sending messages to one another, each a copy of the last, each progressively distorted. As the pages grow blank, the fax and photocopier keep talking. All they do is agree with each other. I am disappearing.

```
Scribo ergo sum. Scribo ergo sum. Scribo ergo
sum.
     The photocopier is real. The fax machine is
real. The robot converses to them. They do not
acknowledge him. Therefore, the robot is not
real.
```

I'm hesitant to try this again. I pick up the receiver and hit numbers at random. It rings.
    "Hello?"
    It is a cheerful voice. My throat grows dry.
    "Hello?" she says.
    I can't remember how to hang up.
    "You know, that's a pretty strange way to use a telephone,

dialing someone's number and then not talking to them."

"Hi. Hi. I'm sorry. I'm not used to talking."

"Oh! Hello! Hello, strange man! So there is someone there after all. Do you know what the first thing anyone ever said on the telephone was?"

I think for a moment. "Was it 'Hello?'"

"No, it was 'Watson, come here. I need you.' That was Alexander Graham Bell, the inventor of the telephone, speaking to his assistant. Do you know why he said it?"

"No, I don't."

"Oh, come on."

"I really don't."

"Take a guess."

"Well...do you think...do you think maybe he was lonely?"

"That sounds likely! I'll bet that while he was inventing he got lonely, so he asked Watson to come and spend some time with him."

"Do you think Watson came?"

"I'm nearly certain he did."

We talk about palindromes, the first dog in outer space, and the Canadian labour movement from 1902-1960. Her human voice speaks directly to me. She's talking about elevators now. Apparently, inside each elevator is a console with a set of buttons on it. Once you step inside and turn around, the console will either be on your left or your right. She says she has an unerring tendency to turn the wrong way, so elevators should have a console on both sides so you can turn in either direction, or at least a mirror at the back so you can know for sure what side it's on.

"I don't like elevators either," I say. "And I'm twenty floors underground!"

"Oh no! Do you turn around too fast and strain your neck? That always happens to me!"

"No. I mean, I don't think I've ever been in an elevator before."

"Well how do you leave?"

"Leave where?"

"The place where you are."

"I'm always in the same place as where I am."

"Do you ever leave?"

I feel no need to answer this. A few moments pass in silence.

She says "Hi."

"Hello," I reply, but she's already hung up.

I don't remember what numbers I pressed to talk to her.

The job of the robot is in danger due to new
holographic workers. The robot lives in a
robot house with his robot girl. He pushes
numbers on his telephone and she speaks to
him. She is nicer than the printer and the fax
machine, and when he speaks to her she listens
and responds to his voice.

Something enters my office. I duck down behind my desk and try to determine what it is. 65% oxygen, 18.8% carbon, 9.5% hydrogen, 3.3% nitrogen, 1.5% calcium, 1% phosphorus, plus potassium, sulphur, chlorine, sodium, magnesium, and traces of iron, fluoride, iodine, and zinc. She has blue eyes.

"You can actually analyze my atomic makeup?" The human has the same voice as the one on the telephone.

"Can't everyone?"

Apparently, different people can analyze different things. For me, it's atomic makeup. For her, it's personalities.

She asks, "Do you know what your personality is?"

"Sure, of course I do."

"Okay then, tell me what it is."

"What? No, you just said you know them. If that's true, why do you need me to say it?"

"Just because I know doesn't mean I tell. It's better for

people to discover it for themselves. You don't know yours."

"Oh no, oh no. I know."

"Okay then. Prove it."

"…"

"See? And you're telling me you know it. You poor thing, you don't even know your own name."

"Yes I do."

"What is it?"

"My name? I have one…I just can't describe it."

"See? I can say my name. It's Clarisse. You don't know your name."

"How do I find out?"

"Do you have any identification? Health card?"

"No."

"Birth certificate?"

"No."

"Driver's licence? Never mind. I don't suppose you have a pay stub."

"I don't even know what a pay stub is."

"You'll have to talk to your boss about that, get it figured out. Where's his office? Do you know?"

"Let's deal with that later."

"No, let's deal with that now."

Clarisse reaches toward me and I take her hand. It is warm and soft. It is somewhat similar to my own body, but it exists outside of me and moves autonomously. Her fingertips touch my palm as she leads me through my office door and out onto the twentieth floor. The fax machine, the photocopier and the telephone become further away. I wave goodbye to them.

It is the unofficial year of the robot.
Unofficial robots ride in unofficial floats
down unofficial metal streets. Mayorbot gives
a speech, off the record, under his breath, in
the shower.

"See? There you go! Just like a little Jacques Cartier!"

I look at Clarisse. I look out at the twentieth floor. The ceiling is pale and fluorescent. The floors are waxy green marble. The hallway seems polite, but there are corridors we might get lost in. We turn left. I'm worried that we won't be able to find my office again. We turn right. I recall Clarisse's unerring tendency to turn the wrong way. Maybe we should be unwinding a string or leaving a trail of crumbs. We turn right. As we wander, I ask questions.

"Before you hung up the phone you said Hi to me. Why did you do that?"

"Oh, that? I figure, why save Hi for the beginning of the next conversation? Hawaiians say Aloha at both the beginning and the end of a conversation. So why not say Hi at the end? It's silly not to, really."

"After you hung up, how did you find me?"

"Oh, I'm resourceful. It's a little thing called wanting to get something done and doing it."

Clarisse wants to talk to my boss. I wonder who he is and if he cares about me. I wonder if I will know him when I see him.

And as they wandered through the tin forest, Robot Boy and the Robot Girl came upon a house built of bread and roofed with cakes, and windows of transparent sugar.

Robot Girl said, "We will have some of this and make a fine meal. It will taste so, so sweet."

Just then the silvery sky was swept with clouds and the Minotaur emerged and ate them alive the end.

We discover a set of large metal doors. Beside them, there is a button with an arrow on it, pointing up.

I ask, "Is this where the boss lives?"

"Nope. This is an elevator."

"We don't have to go in it, do we?"

"No no no. We still have more rooms to see on this floor." She starts walking and I follow.

"Clarisse? You said you can analyze personalities, right?"

"Yep."

"What's yours?"

"Oh mine? 25% grass and leaves and trees, 22% lioness, 17% perpetual motion, 11% angelhair pasta, 9% a bulb's light and 7.5% flakes of snow, plus lesser parts vernal equinox, Gautama Buddha, Nellie McClung, and EP singles. Trace amounts of uranium, the colour orange, the Velvet Underground, and the Adelie Penguin's mating stone."

"Clarisse?"

"Yes?"

"I like your clothes."

She makes a sound like a blackbird makes, something musical.

"Oh, that's laughter," she says.

Laughter equals chirp. Therefore, girl equals bird.

As we progress beyond the elevator, the floor begins to lose its waxy polish. The air is beginning to feel stagnant. We turn left again, left again, right. I can't remember these directions anymore. We reach a brown door with a silvery knob. Inside, there are porcelain basins fitted with chrome handles and levers. There is also a broken mirror, shattered vestiges of glass in the frame. Shards cover the floor. "The boss may have been here." Clarisse checks the garbage can for clues.

I look at my reflection in the slivers.

"Clarisse?"

"Yeah?"

"What's my personality?"

"Are you sure you want to know?"

"Yes, Clarisse. Tell me."

"31% closed doors, 16% brown jacket, 12.5% the letter 'W,' 9% correction fluid, 7% melting ice, and 5.5% Rene Descartes, plus lesser parts of hardcover textbooks, windy streets, and Kilgore Trout. Plus, trace amounts of a full moon, the chirping of a bird, kaleidoscopes, rainbows, and one shadowplay. What do you think?"

"I think I get it."

"That's good. Sometimes they're hard to get."

"Clarisse?"

"Yep?"

"Do you think maybe the letter W is my name?"

"Do you think it's your name?"

"Maybe."

"Then maybe it is."

"Clarisse?"

"Yeah?"

"Is my name pronounced 'double-you' or 'Wwwwwwwww'?"

She chirps.

Crossing the finish line, Marathonbot is hailed by the media and by millions of fanbots who have come from all over the world. Lord Mercury Secundus asks him, "So how does it feel to win?"

"Victory is hard-coded into me. In infinite marathons I would be infinite times victorious. Every victory yields the same emotion, as predetermined by my creator. I cannot defy my programming.

"Also, I would describe the emotion as a particularly positive one."

As we continue through the maze of halls, we come across an open area. There is a desk with paper, pens, sticky notes, and a lamp, all shrouded in a dusty grey substance. The floor is carpeted, and the chair is ergonomic.

"I used to work in one of these, as a receptionist," Clarisse states.

I wonder what else she's done.

"Well I've been an actress, a teacher, an astronomer, a poet, a tree planter, a web designer, a farmer, a checkout girl, a painter, a waitress, a fashion designer, an economist, a gardener, and a biologist. Before that, I was a baby, and before that a sperm and ovum, and then I was an angel, and before that I was an Amazon princess and Hippolyta was my lover and we braided each other's hair and before that I was a lioness and before that I was a tree!"

"And what are you now?"

"A girl who's helping you find your boss. What are you, W?"

"A rainbow. A shadowplay-writing rainbow."

The robots hold a high school dance. State-sanctioned dance events help to reduce incidences of unmonitored youth activity.

Therefore, there is a dance.

At the dance, girlbots and boybots are expressly forbidden to intermingle. Their magnetic chips are polarized to ensure that no boybot and girlbot can get within a three-foot radius of each other.

Green dress bot walks into the gymnasium. I fall in love with her. She falls in love with me. We dance exactly 36 inches apart, gazing at each other across the divide.

When the boybots begin to stick to one another (girlbots likewise), the magnetic chips must be recalibrated. We are demagnet-

ized by remote. The field is neutralized.
During this moment, boy and girl move
together, our bodies gently touching.

The halls turn twisty, serpentine. The walls begin to resemble sandstone. Clarisse slides back a heavy slab to expose a new room: dusty, silent, ruinous. It is singularly ill-lit, and I can only see the outlines of a large oval table surrounded by chairs.

"I can't see anything," I say.

Clarisse lights a match. There is a white sheet hanging from the wall: a projection screen, as Clarisse describes it. The match illuminates nothing else in particular.

"This is called a board-room," says Clarisse. "This is where they used to make their plans." Her match burns out. She heads back to the maze and I follow her.

"Was the boss here?" I ask.

"Many times, I assume. But not recently at all."

"Clarisse?"

"Yeah?"

"Were you really a scientist?"

"Of course I was. You know, I bet you'd really enjoy science."

"Really?"

"Oh yes. Science is the language of love. Take the telophase of mitosis, for example, when cells divide. After the microtubules withdraw, when each daughter's swelling chromatin is wrapped in a thin nuclear envelope, that's when it happens. The cytoplasm spreads open sweetly. The cell membrane advances, presses in tight. Oh, W, it presses so tight. One body becomes two, each pressed up real close against the other."

I melt back into the table, leaning on my elbows. She drifts into me. Her top lip is fair and freckled. Her bottom lip is the softest thing I have ever touched. Our mouths open and close. Her breath is a tender leaf I have never tasted.

I take a moment to recover. In my mind, I tell my friends. See what I just did? I just kissed Clarisse! Twice, three times! The fax machine tells me I can't count the same kiss more than once. Even though I experienced the moment in three temporal states (being about to kiss, kissing, having kissed), I can only count it once. Thermodynamically speaking, no two kisses can occupy the same space at the same time.

So I kiss Clarisse again. That'll show the fax machine. But as my mouth touches hers, nothing else matters. Her lips are everything. Her breath is everything.

```
And he did ascend to the robot plateau, where
before his eyes appeared a burning bush. And
though the bush did live within the flame, it
was not consumed by fire.
    "Another hologram," thought he.
    "Wrong!" spake Godbot.
    The robot trembled and hid his face.
    "Oh, by the way," Godbot did add, "here are
some rules you probably ought to start follow-
ing. One: thou shalt have no other Bots, etc."
```

The filthy corridor starts to slope downward, subtly at first, and then sharply. There are echoes, buzzes, creaks. The air is nearly too thin to breathe. The hall runs down into thick darkness. There could be anything down there.

"Clarisse, don't make me."

She walks into the black void and flicks a switch. A light-bulb turns on, exposing a small door at the hallway's end. She opens it and I run to her, following her through it.

Inside, everything is fresh. The air is the purest I have ever breathed. There are stacks of paper, stacks of boxes, stacks of equipment, stacks of everything! Clarisse begins searching through boxes. "These are all empty," she curses.

I sit on a stack of cardboard sheets, watching her movements. She locates a small metal case, sealed with a lock.

"W!"

She shakes it and hears something moving within. She tries to pull it open with her hands. Failing this, she shakes the box again.

"Clarisse," I say. "I think I understand what you mean about the language of love."

"Huh?"

"The universe expands and contracts. Your lungs expand and contract. Therefore, your breath is the essence of the universe."

"Oh W."

For eons the yangbot has searched for enlightenment. And there she stands: yinbot on the moon. Why did he never look to that orb, that eternal white circle? Has she been there forever? He flies to her on jetboots, kisses her ears, she kisses his eyes, their chi the fuel of perpetual motion.

"Clarisse, I like these stacks of things."

"Me too."

"Clarisse, I would like to stack you on top of me."

"I would like that too."

And so we create each other.

Imagine the caress of metal on metal. Imagine their embrace.

We are in the supply-room, we are among the stacks, we are on the twentieth floor, we are in a meadow under a summer sky.

Robot tree planters plant robot trees. Treebots grow. Sunbot shines. Breezebot blows. Earthbot turns. Dancebots sway. Touchbots

touch. Kissbots kiss. Lovebots love.
Everything is as it should be under Godbot's
blue heaven.

She winds around me. I wear her like an avatar. My spirit
inhabits her body. Inside her I am becoming.

The skyrocket soars. "We've reached infinity,
captain." The engineer presses the "mission
complete" button, deploying 200 million robots
into the centre of the universe. Captain and
crew power down, switch to autopilot, and
rest, and sleep, and sleep.

Hours later, I wake up. I wake up in my office. I look beside
me. I look around me. Clarisse is gone. I search my office. I
search the halls. I search every room on this floor. There is
nothing. There is no evidence that she ever existed. I conduct
a series of experiments to discover her. The results are not
particularly promising.

Experiment 1: A blackbird lands at my imagi-
nary window. She is a pleasure, ocular and
auditory. She teaches me a melody, allows me
to find counterpoint. When I turn my head, she
is gone. Therefore, the blackbird outside my
window does not exist.

Experiment 2: You walk into my office. I
really like you. Therefore, you do not exist.

Experiment 3: You do not exist. I believe that
you exist. I do not exist.

I sleep again. I wake. I sleep again. I wake. I eat bread. As I
am chewing crust it occurs to me that, for a rainbow, I've

never performed a shadowplay. I cast a white curtain over the door, give directions to the cast and crew.

The fax machine and photocopier provide light for a thunderstorm. A wanderer, played by me, journeys through the forest, protecting himself from the rain. I am shaking uncooked rice in an aluminum tray to make the sound.

The telephone provides the sound of a blackbird, illuminated by the lights of heaven. Calmed by gentle chirping, the rain subsides.

The wanderer bows down in worship of the glorious miracle.

The blackbird soars from its perch and scratches out the wanderer's eyes. The white curtain is splattered with red ink.

I flail my arms, scream my throat raw, rip out handfuls of hair, tear down the curtain.

Clarisse is gone. She has left nothing for me.
   And she is everywhere.
   Before Clarisse, humans built no house of brick to repel the sun, but dwelt ant-like in ditches. Clarisse taught humans mathematics, wisdom's lore, and written language. Who, before Clarisse, made canvas wings for sea-battered ships? What human, fallen ill, did not simply shrivel up and die for lack of care? Who dared claim the material hidden deep in the earth: copper, iron, silver, even gold? No-one! So, to put it in a word, every human art, every science, every belief and every thought comes from Clarisse. The best parts of my collection are what she's left behind.

"Nice show, silly."
   "Clarisse?"
   "So, I went and got a crowbar. Should we open the box?"

boop boop beep?

I'd forgotten about the box. Clarisse pries the lid and splits it in two. A sheet of paper drifts to the ground.

"Does this look familiar?" she asks, handing it over.

I read it. I read it more than once.

"Let's leave this place."

I walk resolutely down the sterile hall, step through the elevator doors, and turn toward the console.

"Each of these buttons can take us to a different place."

The doors close.

I am taking nothing with me. I have left one thing behind. There it is, on my desk.

```
From: W
To: The Boss
Cc: Photocopier, Fax Machine, Telephone
Re: Final Report and Resignation


Dear _____,
The boss is not in the office today. He is on
a golf trip. He is home sick. He is at a
Perpetual General Meeting (PGM).
    The boss declares that four score ago all
robots were created equal.
    The boss sends secret messages to the neon
man from mars.
    The boss is the curtain upon which we proj-
ect shadows.
    The boss is on fire, his body the fuel for
the continuing history of our world. Watch the
flames radiate!
    The boss is dead. The boss remains dead.
What is this building, if not his tomb and
monument?
```

ROSEANNE HARVEY currently lives in Montreal, where she is the editor of *ascent magazine*. Since completing her BFA at the University of Victoria, she has lived in England, Japan and a yoga ashram in southeastern BC. She has published both fiction and creative non-fiction in *subTerrain, Geist, Fireweed* and *Goodgirl*.

LARRY BROWN lives in Brantford, Ontario. He has attended the University of Iowa's fiction workshops and his stories have appeared in a number of magazines, including *The Antigonish Review, The Malahat Review, The Fiddlehead* and *The New Quarterly*. He likes Hawaiian shirts, the Habs and The Dave Holland Quintet.

JOEL KATELNIKOFF grew up in Saskatoon, received an MA in creative writing from UNB and now lives in Edmonton. He has published stories in a wide variety of literary journals. His current obsessions include line-jumpers, the 71/72 O-Pee-Chee hockey-card checklist, and the shifting pull of gravity on chrome spheres.

MARK ANTHONY JARMAN has published two collections of stories, *New Orleans Is Sinking* and *19 Knives*, and a travel book, *Ireland's Eye*. His hockey novel *Salvage King Ya!* is on Amazon.ca's list of 50 Essential Canadian Books, and he has won the Gold Medal at the National Magazine Awards. He is the fiction editor of *Fiddlehead* and teaches at UNB.

Previous volumes in this series contained stories by the following writers:

2005: Barbara Romanik, J.M. Villaverde, Jasmina Odor
2004: Neil Smith, Maureen Bilerman, Jaspreet Singh
2003: Liam Durcan, Andrea Rudy, Jessica Grant
2002: Chris Labonté, Lawrence Mathews, Kelly Cooper
2001: J.A. McCormack, Ramona Dearing, Goran Simic
2000: Christine Erwin, Vivette J. Kady, Timothy Taylor
1999: Marcus Youssef, Mary Swan, John Lavery
1998: Leona Theis, Gabriella Goliger, Darryl Whetter
1997: Elyse Gasco, Dennis Bock, Nadine McInnis
1996: Lewis DeSoto, Murray Logan, Kelley Aitken
1995: Warren Cariou, Marilyn Gear Pilling, François
      Bonneville
1994: Donald McNeill, Elise Levine, Lisa Moore
1993: Gayla Reid, Hannah Grant, Barbara Parkin
1992: Caroline Adderson, Marilyn Eisenstat, Marina
      Endicott
1991: Ellen McKeough, Robert Majzels, Patricia Seaman
1990: Peter Stockland, Sara McDonald, Steven Heighton
1989: Brian Burke, Michelle Heinemann, Jean Rysstad
1988: Christopher Fisher, Carol Anne Wien, Rick Hillis
1987: Charles Foran, Patricia Bradbury, Cynthia Holz
1986: Dayv James-French, Lesley Krueger, Rohinton
      Mistry
1985: Sheila Delany, Frances Itani, Judith Pond
1984: Diane Schoemperlen, Joan Fern Shaw, Michael
      Rawdon
1983: Sharon Butala, Bonnie Burnard, Sharon Sparling
1982: Barry Dempster, Don Dickinson, Dave Margoshes
1981: Peter Behrens, Linda Svendsen, Ernest Hekkanen
1980: Martin Avery, Isabel Huggan, Mike Mason

Most of these books are still available. Please inquire.